Contents

Series Preface

The book you have before you is part of a three-volume series on using the Bible in pastoral practice.

The series is the fruit of a partnership between Bible Society and the School of Religious and Theological Studies at Cardiff University. Bible Society wants to make the voice of the Bible heard everywhere; this project aims to develop critical awareness of the ways in which the Bible is, and might better be, used in pastoral practice.

We take pastoral practice to be the activity of Christians that nurtures flourishing in all areas of human life – individual, ecclesiastical and social. So it might include campaigning against world debt, managing health-care organisations, chairing congregational meetings, preaching, taking school assemblies, neighbourhood visiting, bereavement counselling and conducting weddings, amongst many other activities. Pastoral practice thus widely defined includes the activities of lay people and clergy.

The project group's working assumption is that the Bible pertains, or should pertain, directly and indirectly to all pastoral activities. However, there seems to be little specific knowledge of how the Bible is actually used, or systematic consideration as to how it might be used better. So one of our aims has been actually to document the ways in which the Bible is and might be used.

A summary report of this preliminary empirical investigation, carried out by a specially appointed Fellow of the University, can be found on the School of Religious Studies website at Cardiff University (www.cardiff.ac.uk). This has been supplemented by historical and theoretical explorations in the practical interpretation of the Bible. One outcome of the project is the production of three books which, severally and together, should enable those involved in pastoral practice to analyse their own present use of the Bible and to learn how to use it more creatively.

The first of these books, *The Bible in Practice*, provides a rich overview of the ways in which Christians have, and could, use the Bible in their pastoral work. In *Holy Bible, Human Bible*, Gordon Oliver presents a personal view of the way in which the Bible challenges pastoral practice and pastoral practice challenges understandings of the Bible. The present, final book, *Using the Bible in Christian Ministry: A Workbook* draws upon empirical research undertaken within the project as well as on the other two volumes. This should enable practitioners to review, evaluate, and, if they wish, to change their use of the Bible in their everyday life and work. The book is based upon the experience and practice of many different people and is intended to make a real difference to the ways in which practitioners view and use the Bible and enable others to interact with the Bible. It thus provides a creative and critical source for ministry.

As series editors, we are grateful to the editors, authors and contributors to all the books and to our publishers. If this volume and its companions succeed in opening up more critical and creative opportunities for the Bible in pastoral practice at all levels, then all the work that has been done will have been well worth while.

David Spriggs, Bible Society
Stephen Pattison, Cardiff University
Series Editors

Acknowledgements

Many people have contributed to this workbook in its planning, writing and publication. It is in every way a corporate effort and it is impossible to mention everyone who has helped to make it what it is.

At the planning stage the book was guided by members of the Cardiff University/Bible Society 'Use of the Bible in Pastoral Practice' Project Steering Group and members of that group have continued to comment on its various drafts in its progress towards publication. Ian Dickson did most of the basic research upon which the genesis of the book was founded. Others who contributed to special planning meetings from outside the project include Peter Cruchley-Jones, Judith Thompson and Andrew Todd, who also contributed the activity on pages 22–3.

At the drafting stage, we are particularly grateful to David Muir for his insightful comments. We would also like to thank the following people for their help in trialling the book:

Diane Bruckland, Sonia Barron, Martha Clark, Jonathan Clark, Daniel Cooling, Marcellina Cooney, Dave Cordrey, Wendy Davies, Elizabeth Dunning, Deborah Helme, Simon Helme, Diane Hudson, Rachel Hudson, Chris Hudson, Rob James, Jane Kenchington, Sylvia Law, Susan Marchant, Mary Jo Martin, David Muir, Rosie Marks, George Oliver, Meg Oliver, Ruth Steggles, Stephen Travis, Chris Rankin, Jacqueline Rodwell, Nigel Rooms, Sally Smith, Tom Wallace, Euros Wyn Jones, Anne Zeiss

Malcolm Laverty is the artist responsible for the cartoon on page 138. The publishers would welcome any information enabling them to contact Malcolm Laverty as they have been unable to do so.

We are grateful to Darton, Longman and Todd, and particularly to Virginia Hearn, their commissioning editor, for supporting and being so enthusiastic about this book and its two siblings in the current series.

The Steering Group of the Cardiff University/Bible Society 'Use of the Bible in Pastoral Practice' Project would like to thank Margaret Cooling and Trevor Cooling for their providentially arriving to be the main writers of this work at just the right time.

Making the most of this workbook

When embarking on a book like this, it is important to spend a little time making sure you know how to make the most of it. You probably have your own ideas about what you want to gain from it. Spending a short time reading these introductory sections should help you to achieve your aims and prevent misunderstandings.

Introduction to the workbook

The Bible is a major resource for all aspects of Christian life and work. However, use of the Bible in Christian ministry is more often assumed than examined.

This workbook will help you to reflect upon, and improve, your use of the Bible in Christian ministry. It offers models and techniques that could inform your practice. It will take you through a number of issues. With reflection, you will be able to come to your own conclusions concerning what is good practice. By the time you finish, you should have a deeper understanding of the ways in which you and others actually use the Bible in ministry. You should also be able to see and plan how you might use it differently, if that is your wish.

Active involvement

This is not a book to be read then replaced on the shelves like a novel. It is a workbook, designed to help you learn about and reflect in depth on your own experience. In effect, you are going to write your own book on how you think you use the Bible and how you might want to change that use. You therefore become a co-author by the way you reflect and write your responses. If you tackle the activities, the book will stretch you and you should learn a lot about your own ministry.

Pastoral care/mission

This book focuses mainly on the pastoral dimension of ministry. However, it does *not* seek to turn the reader inward or only towards personal and local issues. Nor is it about the church 'servicing itself' and disregarding the rest of the world. It is about equipping people to pastor each other and turn outwards to their neighbours. Pastoral care is a form of mission. This book aims to promote reflection on different uses of the Bible so that Christian ministry and mission are exercised creatively.

Background to the workbook

The research project

This book arises out of a joint research project between Bible Society and Cardiff University. This tried to identify how people do, and could, use the Bible appropriately in ministry and pastoral practice. Some of the ideas and activities in this book are based on survey work undertaken as part of the research. You can find out more about the research project and its results by looking at the Cardiff University website (www.cardiff.ac.uk/relig) and in other materials arising from the project:

a. the Reader: Paul Ballard and Stephen R. Holmes (eds), *The Bible in Pastoral Practice; Readings in the Place and Function of Scripture in the Church*, Darton Longman and Todd, (2005)

b. a more 'popular' book: Gordon Oliver, *Holy Bible, Human Bible: Questions Pastoral Practice Must Ask,* Darton Longman and Todd (2006)

c. an article by Ian Dickson: 'The Bible in Pastoral Ministry: The Quest for Best Practice', *Journal of Adult Theological Education* 4.1 April 2007, 102–19.

References to the research project in the text are indicated by the term 'research project'. Other research will be referenced according to its source and date.

Christian ministry and/or pastoral practice?

The title of this book includes the words 'Christian ministry', but throughout the book you will see the phrase 'pastoral practice' used interchangeably with it. There are several reasons for this:

◆ In this book pastoral practice is defined widely to encompass most Christian ministry. In his book *A Critique of Pastoral Care* Stephen Pattison defines pastoral care as:

> *that activity, undertaken especially by representative Christian persons, directed towards the elimination and relief of sin and sorrow and the presentation of all people perfect in Christ to God (2000, p13).*

Pastoral ministry might be *especially* the responsibility of certain people within the church, but it is not *exclusively* so. Often the role of that person or team will be to equip, enable and encourage others, and to act as a point around which others gather; a centre of standards, inspiration and training.

◆ In the research project pastoral practice was defined as:

> *the whole gamut of Christian ministry related to the comprehensive needs of other human beings, whether Christian or not.*

Many people define pastoral practice more narrowly (e.g. listening ministry, care and visiting, etc.) but that is only an element of this book (units 8 and 9). It was therefore appropriate to use a different term to cover the wide range of contexts that this book addresses.

◆ The pastoral is one way of viewing the whole of Christian ministry; most ministries have a pastoral aspect.

◆ Pastoral theology deals with human experience and every aspect of life, so pastoral practice should be equally wide in its scope.

Who is the workbook for?

This workbook is designed *primarily* for those who have some familiarity with theology and ministry. It offers an overview of important topics, emphasising reflection on practice through undertaking activities and reviewing case studies. The style is 'to the point', with brief sections; there are plenty of things for you to work at. It is not a textbook, nor does it offer detailed scholarly treatment of the topics (though it is substantially based on scholarship). Rather, it is a tool for creating a learning experience. Probably the user will already be familiar with some, if not all, of the material. The value of the book lies in the way it brings together theory and practice. You will benefit most from doing the exercises rather than reading the text.

The workbook's purpose is to raise confidence in the use of the Bible in day-to-day ministry and it draws on the research literature with that purpose in mind. It is anticipated that church leaders will find it helpful:

◆ in reviewing their own thinking and practice.
◆ as a tool for use with others they help to train for pastoral ministry.

Note: the term 'pastor' is often used within the book to indicate the person giving pastoral care; that person need not be a clergyperson or other officially recognised office holder, but will probably have some leadership function within a church.

For individuals and for groups

The workbook can be used by an individual working alone or with a group. You should choose your own appropriate purpose. For example, the material could be used for formal lay leadership training or by a group of friends getting together to further their own thinking. Individual and group activities are provided throughout; you can choose which you want to undertake. Some of the group activities will also work for individuals. However, this is not intended as general housegroup material, although it could be used for training housegroup leaders. When used in a group the leaders should remember that some of the activities explore personal perspectives; this material needs sensitive handling.

Photocopying

The purchaser has permission to make photocopies of appropriate parts of the book necessary for the activity, for use in group work. No copyright material can be photocopied.

As part of a taught course

This book can play a role in a taught course, for example, for those in ministerial training or on a theology degree. It could provide an input into courses on pastoral practice, the Bible and Christian ministry and can be used:

◆ as a stimulus for planning the structure of a course.
◆ to supplement a course, for example as a source of backup/private study material.
◆ to provide activities for use with individual students or in active learning group exercises.

How to use the workbook – creating your own learning experience

The distinctive feature of this workbook is that it asks you, the user, to become a co-author. It acts as a resource to dip into, enabling you to engage in a personal learning experience. You will fulfil your particular needs through the units you choose to study and the order in which you study them. So it is important to spend a little time planning how you will use it. We suggest the following:

Step 1: Familiarise yourself with the book

Spend a few minutes browsing the pages of the workbook. There are 15 units and a final summary. These are divided into four sections:

Section 1: Units 1–3

This section covers the basics. You will review your current use of the Bible, your understanding of the nature of the Bible and your thinking about the nature of Christian ministry.

Section 2: Units 4–8

This section covers crucial background issues. You will consider the authority and interpretation of the Bible, what sort of book it is and how people respond to it differently.

Section 3: Units 9–15

This section covers a range of different pastoral contexts. You will explore practical issues relating to the use of the Bible in each of them.

Section 4: Unit 16

This section enables you to review what you have learnt and to develop a personal action plan.

Step 2: Complete Unit 1

Unit 1 will support you in reviewing your current use of the Bible. We recommend that you study it first as a way of identifying your own training needs. This will act as a marker for your subsequent learning and development.

Step 3: Identify some goals

In the light of your study of unit 1, identify some personal goals. Examples might be:

◆ to update my understanding of the literature on the nature of the Bible.
◆ to use a new method of communication.
◆ to review my use of the Bible with children.
◆ to develop creative ways of using the Bible in small groups.

Step 4: Plan and prioritise your personal curriculum

It might help to think of the workbook as a corridor with many doors to open, behind which are rooms to explore. Having identified your needs and goals, you need to design a curriculum of your own. You can use the key question at the start of each unit to try each door and have a peek inside the room. This will enable you to identify those units that are most relevant to your identified needs. Then decide an order for studying them. This will depend on:

◆ your own personal priorities.
◆ your judgment as to the order of study that will best help you to fulfil your goals.

The case study below gives an example of the process.

Bob Jones has been in pastoral ministry in a full-time capacity for 15 years. This is his second church. Having worked through unit 1 he has identified the following needs and goals.

◆ *His academic theological training was some time ago. He needs to refresh this.*
◆ *Outreach to the housing estate where his church is located has been identified as a priority in the church's medium-term plan. Bob feels both he and his congregation need to think very carefully about how they communicate with people who have never been inside church.*
◆ *To him, his preaching feels dry, predictable and safe. He feels that both he and the congregation need to challenge themselves.*

Bob therefore makes the following decisions about how he will use the workbook.

◆ *He will set aside one week as an intensive personal study week to focus on units 4, 5 and 6 as a way of revitalising his own understanding of theological debates about the nature and use of the Bible. He will spend one day working through the three units and then four days in his local theological college library to follow up the resources lists.*
◆ *He will work through units 7, 10, 13 and 14 over the summer in preparation for developing an action plan for the outreach with the other church leaders. He will select activities to use in group work with the other leaders.*
◆ *He will then skim unit 15 as a way of thinking about creative forms of communication.*
◆ *He will review his preaching by making unit 6 the focus of his sermon preparation for a four-week series in the winter on Challenging Texts from the Bible.*

In planning your own curriculum, the skill will be in identifying those units that contribute to meeting your priorities. This will mean skimming the units. For example, if your priority is to improve your work with children, units 10 and 14 are obvious choices. But the following would also potentially be very helpful:

> unit 7, as exploring metaphor is an important dimension of work in schools.
> unit 8, as recognising individual difference is a priority for teachers.
> unit 15, as the creative arts are on the educational agenda.

So be creative in your use of the workbook. You could, of course, aim to cover the whole book to ensure that you missed nothing relevant. This will maximise the value of the book to you.

Remember, you don't have to cover all units in the same depth. You might undertake all the activities and reflections and follow up the resources list in a unit. However, you could skim the text in about 10 minutes. It is up to you!

A tip for making the most of your own learning experience

Before you begin your study, decide how you are going to keep notes of your own work. This will include your responses to activities, your thoughts along the way, and your reflections. You need to capture these at the time to gain long-term benefit from your study. We suggest you use:

1. a consecutive notebook in which you write responses.
2. notes on the workbook itself (if it is your copy!).
3. a reflective diary.

Overlaps

In places, there is a small amount of overlap between units. This is inevitable when trying to create self-contained units that may also be read as part of a whole book. If you come across an area of overlap, that can be skimmed.

Timing

Each unit is designed to take up to three hours but people work at different rates. If you think it will take you more than three hours but you don't have that time available then you might wish to reflect on some activities rather than doing them in detail. Occasionally there is an activity that will take more than the three hours, e.g., keeping a weekly log of Bible use or taking some notes during a sermon. If you are in a group context when you are likely to have less than three hours, you should select from the sections within a unit.

Cross referencing

Throughout the units you will find there is cross referencing. Looking up these references will enrich your study, but it is not essential.

Things you might need

It is helpful to have access to the following: pens, pencils, paper (different sizes), glue sticks, highlighters, post-it notes, erasers and scissors. We will notify you of anything additional to these that you might need at the start of the unit.

The structure of a unit

Each unit comprises the following elements.

Key question

A key question begins each unit. This provides a clear sense of focus. The question encapsulates the main learning experience for the unit. Each unit is divided into sections, with each section contributing a distinct perspective on the key question. By the end of any unit, you should have something to say in response to the key question.

Activities

Each unit has a number of learning activities. Most have been designed so you can complete them in one sitting, although occasionally you will have to break the study session to finish an activity or collect some things together beforehand. A few activities, for example, interviewing a friend or taking notes on a sermon, can only be undertaken outside the study session. Look ahead before starting a unit to identify anything you might need to collect together or prepare in advance. Notes on any preparation needed are given on the first page of each unit.

Within any unit, activities are numbered according to the section in which they occur. For example in section 4 of unit 6 the activity will be numbered **Activity 4**. Both individual and group activities are supplied and readers can select which they use.

(I) indicates an activity designed for individuals

 (G) indicates an activity designed for a group

 (I/G) indicates an activity that can be used by groups or individuals.

There are sometimes optional activities; glance ahead to check if you want to do these.

 ## Feedback

Feedback is given for most of the activities. This allows you to see the sort of responses others have made. It is not meant to be a 'right answer' against which you check your own. Looking at the feedback may help you to grasp the activity quickly. Sometimes the feedback covers part and not the whole activity because of space. The feedback is provided by a number of people, including the authors. It does not necessarily represent the authors' own views. Sometimes the feedback reflects a compilation of several people's responses. We are grateful to the people who trialled this workbook for their contributions to the feedback.

Case studies

The case studies are frequently based on real incidents that have been fictionalised to protect identity. Often they are formed from composite accounts and experiences. So any apparent reference to persons or situations, past or present, that you might think you recognise is entirely coincidental. Case studies are indicated by a box in the text.

 ## Reflections

Results of the research project indicated that the pressures of pastoral ministry mean that there is little time for regular reflection on how and why the Bible is used. Reflective exercises are included throughout this book and are an integral element of the learning experience it offers. To get the most out of this book, we recommend that you keep a notebook as a reflective diary to record your thoughts.

(You are not required at any point to change your theological position, but you will asked to reflect on your position and how it affects your practice.)

Review

Some possible learning outcomes are summarised at the end of the unit so that you can review what you have achieved at the end of a study session. Of course these represent the authors' ideas and you may well attain different learning outcomes that are more important to you.

Resources

A resources list of books, articles and websites is provided allowing you to follow up a subject in greater depth. All websites were live at the time of writing.

Section 1

The Basics

Unit 1

Understanding my current use of the Bible in pastoral practice

Key question

How do I currently use the Bible in my pastoral practice and what has shaped this use?

Preparation

This unit involves keeping a weekly log of your use of the Bible. You may wish to read activity 1 and prepare your log before you work through the whole unit.

1. Introduction

The Bible comes in many forms: book, electronic and audio. It also comes in many different versions; are you an NRSV user or do you prefer 'The Word on the Street'? Do you like to handle a book, or use the Bible online (see websites)? The research project showed that most people used the Bible in book form and some who did use electronic versions felt the need to apologise for this. One group used the Bible from memory, working with others to build community memories of Bible stories rather than reading from a book.

The version of the Bible we use, and the form it comes in, may influence our use of the text. The contexts in which we use the Bible also affect use; for example, our use of the text in preaching and hospital visiting is likely to differ widely. Spending time in tracking when and how we use the Bible may alert us to discrepancies between our perception of our use of the Bible and what actually happens.

Activity 1 (I): How do you use the Bible in everyday practice?

Create a week's log of your use of the Bible either as a daily diary or from memory. (See the feedback for an example.)

a. Divide a piece of paper into four columns as in the diagram. Create one of these for each day of the week.
b. Under 'Context', note the different contexts in which the Bible was used on that day. Note some contexts where the Bible is not used.
c. Under 'Format/version' write the format you use, e.g. electronic, book form or from memory. If you used a book form, note the version.

   d. Under 'Open/closed', note if the Bible was actually opened or accessed or if it was there as a 'presence'.

   e. Under 'Who used it/How' note who opened and used the Bible. Who read it, quoted from it or used it in some other way?

Activity 1 (G)

As for the individual activity, but at the meeting, group members can share their weekly log with each other and compare notes. Does a pattern emerge?

Feedback

This is my log for Monday. When I looked at the rest of the week, I was surprised to find how often I used the Bible during the week. It's a bigger part of my life than I realised. I never use it on a Friday and Saturday (my days off).

When and in what context?	What format or version?	Was the Bible opened or closed?	Who used it and how?
Monday: Staff meeting.	Book, several versions.	Opened.	Shared Bible study/reflection.
School.	Living Story Bible.	Open.	Me telling Bible stories to primary children.

Reflection

Look back over your log: is there anything surprising? Do you think this week was typical or atypical? Are some contexts 'Bible free zones'? Are other areas 'Bible rich'? Which do you think affects your use of the Bible most: the context, the form or your personal preference? Record your thoughts in your reflective diary.

2. Why am I doing this?

It is important to think about why you are investing time in this workbook. You may have come to it with a variety of expectations; some of these you will be aware of, others you may be below the surface. Whatever form your expectations take, they will influence your attitudes, so it is helpful to clarify what you expect to get out of this book at an early stage.

Activity 2 (I): Why am I doing this?

Imagine this book is a course (which it is not) and there are only a limited number of places available. You are applying for a place on it and you need to answer the following questions:

a. How would you describe yourself and your role in Christian ministry? You might wish to turn to the definition of pastoral practice on page 36 to help you think about this.

b. What is your main reason for engaging in this study?

c. What other reasons do you have for applying for this course?

d. Has anything happened to trigger this interest?

e. What do you hope will be the main outcome?

f. Why do you think your expectations are realistic?

Activity 2 (G)

As for the individual activity, but create individual application forms which people can fill in and discuss.

Feedback

a. My role is one of priest.

b. My main reason for engaging in this study is to gain a better understanding of how I use the Bible.

c. To explore how I use the Bible. Am I using it enough? Am I using it in a variety of ways?

e. I know one book is not going to answer all my questions, but I would like to become more confident in new ways of using the Bible in my ministry.

f. I know that I become more confident once I have had time to think about an issue.

3. Identifying good practice

This book is intended to help you to think about how you currently use the Bible in your ministry and review how you might improve its use. So it is important to establish your own personal starting point. As you begin this book, we are asking you to spend some time in thinking about how you currently use the Bible in your pastoral practice. Awareness of your present practice acts as your benchmark from which to progress your thinking.

Most of us have opinions about how the Bible should be used in pastoral practice even if we have not articulated them. We feel that we know good pastoral practice when we meet it. This next activity is about clarifying what constitutes good practice.

Note: the term 'pastoral practice' is used interchangeably with the phrase 'Christian ministry'. For an explanation of this, please see page 10.

Activity 3 (I): How should the Bible be used in pastoral practice?

Think of a time when you saw, experienced or were involved in good pastoral practice that involved the use of the Bible. Try to work out what made it good practice. Write a series of bullet points (not more than 100 words in total) on what characterises good practice when using the Bible in Christian ministry. Some people find it easier to start by thinking about what is *not* good practice and work from there. When you have finished this book we will come back to this activity to see if you wish to change anything.

Activity 3 (G)

As for the individual activity, but ask members to swap descriptions of good practice and read their neighbour's.

Feedback

In the research project, when describing good practice, practitioners used words such as: 'sensitive', 'respect', 'honest' and 'freedom'. Descriptions of bad practice included words such as 'manipulative', 'detextualised' and 'dominating'.

4. The Bible as a shaper of people

The Bible can shape the way we think, feel and act. It can shape the way we view ourselves, others, the world and God. Before we look at how we use the Bible with others, we need to understand how we ourselves are shaped by the Bible, not only in our pastoral practice but in many other areas of life. This may help us to understand our use of the text. In the research project, some practitioners stressed the formative role of the Bible: the Bible formed the people who in turn ministered to others. That was considered to be one of the influential ways in which the Bible shaped pastoral practice.

Reflection

Look back over your own history and think about the role the Bible has played in shaping you both positively and negatively. Are there any key moments when you remember the Bible being used in a particularly appropriate or inappropriate way? (Did other people in your life feel the Bible was important enough to use it with you? How did you respond to that? Did other people in your life avoid using the Bible with you? Why do you think they did that, and how do you feel about it?) Record your thoughts in your reflective diary.

Activity 4 (I): Expectations and experiences

Look at the words in the box. They are all words that describe the impact the Bible might have on people. If, during the activity, you think of other words you would like to include, just add them to the box.

a. Underline or highlight, in one colour, the words that express *your expectations* concerning the way reading the Bible will affect you.
b. Underline or highlight, in a different colour, the words that express *what happens in reality* when you engage with the Bible.
c. Underline or highlight, in a third colour, those words that express how you were *encouraged to think* of the impact of the Bible as part of your upbringing or education.

Look at the different colours. Are there any patterns in your expectations and responses to the Bible? (Don't worry if no pattern seems to emerge.) For example, you might have been encouraged to think of the Bible as boring by your upbringing but actually found it stimulating so this would give a pattern of opposites. Write a short summary (no more than 100 words) to explain the patterns you observed in your responses to this activity.

Inspire	*Challenge*	*Embarrass*	*Equip*	*Confuse*	*Annoy*
Stimulate	*Move to action*	*Reassure*	*Inform*	*Provoke*	
Shock	*Excite*	*Horrify*	*Guide*	*Move to prayer*	*Bore*
Depress	*Comfort*				

Activity 4 (G)

Follow the individual activity; but the words could be placed on cards on the floor or the table. Group members could take it in turns to pick up a key word/s and explain their choice rather than underline words. Alternatively, they could make a note of their key words for a–c. This could be followed by discussion rather than writing about the emerging patterns.

Option: Picturing the past

Draw a picture (pin people is sufficient) representing an early occasion when you experienced the Bible and choose a colour that you think reflects the feeling and mood of that incident and colour part of the picture. The amount of the picture you colour and how deep it is can reflect the strength of the mood. Alternatively, add words to describe the mood and feelings. If more than one occasion comes to mind you can repeat the activity.

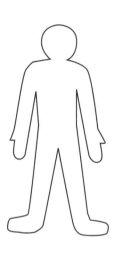

Feedback

These are my responses to this activity:

a. inspire, conspire, challenge, inform, provoke, guide, comfort, move to prayer, excite, move to action, stimulate.
b. challenge, equip, guide, inform, excite, reassure, annoy, stimulate, inspire.
c. inspire, move to prayer, guide, challenge.

My upbringing led me to believe that the Bible would be exciting and useful but as a teenager I found it boring. Since then it has been better than I was led to believe, I feel encouraged and strengthened by what I read.

5. Experiencing the text

Most people in Western society have experienced the Bible in some way. We might have been the one using the Bible with someone else, or we might have been on the 'receiving end' of someone else's use of the text. This experience can be deeply enriching, alarmingly shallow or even abusive. Examining our own experience can help us to understand other people's attitudes towards the Bible and its use.

Reflection

Think back to your own experience of the Bible and identify an instance when the Bible has been used in ways that were enriching; then think of a time when you thought the use was shallow. Have you ever experienced the Bible being used in a way that you thought was abusive? What made it abusive? Record your thoughts in your reflective diary.

6. Reviewing how you understand Bible use

Christians use the Bible in a variety of ways. Sometimes we read from the Bible or quote or paraphrase the text. This use is explicit. At other times our use is less obvious and more implicit; we may use themes from the Bible such as fall and redemption or biblical metaphors such as 'shining as lights'. The Bible can also be our framework for thinking, affecting the way in which we view the world. For example, our attitude towards the less advantaged may reflect the biblical bias towards the poor. As we experience situations, different words, themes and stories may come to mind. For example, I cannot pass someone begging without thinking of the Good Samaritan story.

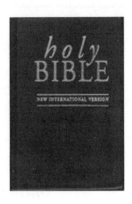

Reflection

Sometimes we see parts of our week as 'Bible poor' because we have defined Bible use very narrowly. However, if we include our implicit as well as our explicit use of the Bible we may see those areas as richer than we previously thought. Look back over your log. How would thinking in these terms change the way you view your Bible use? Record your thoughts in your reflective diary.

7. Reviewing the parts of the Bible you use

Not only are we selective in how and when we use the Bible, we are also selective concerning *which parts* we use. Although Christians believe that the whole Bible is an inspired book, *in practice*, some parts are little used. In effect, most of us create a personal Bible within the whole text of the Bible: our 'canon within the canon'. The lists in Chronicles and the dietary details of Leviticus are not favourite reading for many Christians. Becoming more aware of the parts of the Bible we turn to most often and those we avoid may make us re-examine what we use.

Reflection

Look at your Bible; can you spot your favourite parts just by looking at it? Are some parts more worn, dirty and thumbed than others? Can you explain why? How aware do you think you are of your Bible use? For example, think back over your ministry over the last month: have you used a range of biblical material or do you tend to use the same selection of passages? Are there good reasons for this? Record your thoughts in your reflective diary.

Activity 7 (I/G): What is my indispensable personal and pastoral Bible?

Everyone has favourite parts of the Bible that they find really useful, but we are not always aware of our reasons for liking them. The following activity may help you to explore why you favour certain passages.

a. Imagine you are fleeing the country and you will be in a refugee camp for a long time. You only have time to tear three passages from the Bible to take with you. Which would they be?

b. If the question were changed and you were asked to imagine that you were going to minister as a Christian in that camp for several years but you, too, only have time to tear out the three passages would they be the same three texts? Why? Why not?

c. If you have time you might like to repeat this activity, thinking about your least favourite and three least useful passages.

Option: Bermuda Triangle

This is a group game. Play 'Bermuda Triangle' for c. In this game the contestant has to make a case for a passage from the Bible to be sent to the Bermuda Triangle (a place where things disappear). The host and audience try to dissuade the contestant and present the opposite case. After several minutes (decide on a time) there is a vote and the passage is either sent to the Bermuda Triangle or saved. Group members can rotate being contestants and host.

Feedback

a. I would take the following passages to the refugee camp for my encouragement:

> Revelation 21:1–8
> John 1
> Esther 4

b. I would take the following passages to the camp because they are on the love of God, the Word incarnate and daily living (armour of God) and are useful to teach others:

> 1 Corinthians 13
> Ephesians 6
> John 1

Final reflection

Look back at the key question. How would you answer it now? Think about your ideal use of the Bible and compare it to your actual use as revealed in the work you have done in this unit. Is there a difference? Is it significant? What are the reasons for the difference? Record your thoughts in your reflective diary.

Review

Now you have worked through this unit you should be able to:

◆ explain to yourself what your motives and expectations are in working on this book.
◆ describe your pattern of Bible use in pastoral contexts.
◆ give reasons for your present use of the Bible in Christian ministry.
◆ plan how to use this workbook to best effect.

Final activity

Turn to page 9 and plan how to make best use of this workbook.

Resources

Ballard, P. and Holmes, S. R. (eds) (2005) *The Bible in Pastoral Practice*. Darton, Longman and Todd. Introduction and essay 11.

Ballard, P. and Pritchard, J. (2006) *Practical Theology in Action: Christian Thinking in the Service of Church and Society* (revised edition). SPCK.

Lyall, D. (2001) *The Integrity of Pastoral Care* (New Library of Pastoral Care). SPCK. Chapter 8.

Oliver, G. (2006) *Holy Bible, Human Bible: Questions Pastoral Practice Must Ask*. Darton, Longman and Todd. Chapter 1.

Peterson, E. H. (1980) *Five Smooth Stones for Pastoral Work*. Wm. B. Eerdmans Publishing Co. Introduction.

www.gen.nz
www.bible.com
www.bible.org   } online Bibles
www.biblegateway.com
www.religion-online.org Select 'Ministry'

Unit 2

How does the nature of the Bible affect pastoral practice?

Key question

How does my understanding of the nature of the Bible and the way it shapes people and situations impact on my pastoral practice?

Preparation

You will need some newspapers and magazines for this unit (page 30).

1. Introduction

How we see the Bible affects our use of it in ministry. Christians view the Bible in different ways. Some see it as a story of a relationship, for others it is primarily a guide book for life. The research project showed that few practitioners saw the Bible as a source of proof texts. People tended to think more in terms of the Bible as a 'treasure chest', a 'foundation' and a 'resource' (or *the* resource).

Activity 1 (I): How do you think about the Bible?

Complete the sentences a. and b. by selecting appropriate words from the first box.

a. For me the Bible is primarily …
b. For me the Bible is not really …

A guide   *A text book*   *A pointer to God*   *A story of a friendship*

A foundation on which we stand   *A rule book*   *A drama about God and humanity*

A book of beliefs   *An answer book*   *A love story*   *A manual*

A revelation from God   *A witness*

Complete the sentences c. and d. by selecting appropriate words from the second box.

c. I think the Bible can most fruitfully be used for …
d. I believe the Bible should never be used for …

Guidance	*Comfort*	*Challenging people*	*Intimidating people into faith*
Giving people hope	*Informing people*		*Helping people to live the Christian life*
Controlling people	*Personal devotion*	*Deciding doctrine/beliefs*	*Discipline*

Look at your answers in both boxes and compare them. In what ways do you think your understanding of the nature of the Bible affects the way you use it? Jot down a few sentences.

Activity 1 (G)

Write the incomplete sentences on pieces of card and pass them round for others to complete verbally. The words in the boxes can be displayed on large sheets. Give an example from the feedback or supply your own finished sentences to get people started. Note the degree of variation across the group and discuss how the way in which we view the Bible impacts on our use.

Feedback

a. For me the Bible is primarily a foundation and guide.
b. For me the Bible is not really a rule book or source of holy thoughts.
c. I think the Bible can fruitfully be used for exploring our relationship with God and one another.
d. I believe the Bible should never be used for condemning people or writing them off.

I view the Bible as foundation and guide and useful for exploring relationships. This means that I tend to use it for case histories, self examination and to cast a light on our own relationships, attitudes and behaviour.

2. Allowing the Bible to shape the Church community

Even in the most Bible-based church, the Bible can be unintentionally relegated to the sidelines because its role is narrowly understood. For example, the Bible might be on every chair, but secular theories of management might be adopted to run the church. These theories, based on concepts of target setting and performance indicators, may be used without any critique from biblical perspectives. In contrast, the Bible can have a broad shaping influence, determining beliefs, attitudes, behaviour, organisation and structures within a church. It can do this by providing:

◆ the over-arching story of God's relationship with humanity for the church to share, live and celebrate.
◆ the inspiration and influence that changes people.
◆ stories that help to shape community work, worship and evangelism.
◆ beliefs about God, ourselves, the world and others.
◆ practices to translate into daily life and principles to live and work by.
◆ models of behaviour to look up to (and some others to avoid).

Activity 2 (I): How does the Bible shape your Christian community?

In our society, there are inspectors in all walks of life. Imagine a Bible inspector is coming to your church to assess the influence of the Bible on church life. She/he is going to look at the following areas:

◆ organisation and leadership
◆ work and mission
◆ worship
◆ teaching

Choose one area and write what you think the report might be for that area in not more than 100 words.

Activity (G)

As for the individual activity, but role-play the inspector's visit. One person should adopt the role of the inspector, wearing a badge and carrying a clipboard. Other members of the group represent different areas of church life e.g. worship leader, administrative leader, person in charge of preaching and teaching. The inspector should question each in turn. You might like to discuss the questions the inspector might ask and how people might respond before the role-play begins. The results of the role-play can be used as a basis for discussion. Alternatively, divide the group into pairs. Each pair should select an area of church life and discuss how the Bible shapes it. Each pair can then report to the whole group.

Feedback

Our minister expects people to be in church twice on Sunday and you have to be seen to be busy. There are endless meetings and I think the church motto is 'Busyness is next to godliness'. I think the Bible's teaching on rest, Sabbath and fullness of life has something to say to us.

3. The Bible's role in shaping the wider community

So far we have looked at how the Bible can shape the Christian community, but does the Bible also shape the wider community? Christians often despair that the modern world has lost its Christian foundation; the past is seen as 'Bible rich', but the present is seen as 'Bible poor'. This leaves people unsure about using the Bible in what feels like an alien environment, where people do not understand the language and ideas of the Bible. Bible Society research (*The Use of Scripture*, June 2000) showed that people believed that the Bible has had a strong influence in shaping British culture in terms of values, laws, education and family, but little influence on the media. Although we may be in a

©hris Morgan 1995   cxmedia.com

post-Christian era (scholars differ over this) the influence of the Bible may still be there, even if it is not obvious or acknowledged. The Christianity and Culture project was set up to investigate this claim (www.york.ac.uk/inst/cms/candc/index.html).

Reflection

Think about the way the Bible influences our culture. Flip through some newspapers or magazines: what are your immediate impressions? Look a bit closer: do you see any evidence of the Bible shaping ideas and attitudes?

4. Biblical genres and Christian ministry: using stories

The Bible contains many literary forms, and our awareness of the nature and function of these different genres can help us to use the Bible with integrity in pastoral situations. In this section we will examine story. In the following sections we will examine proverb and parable.

Biblical stories combined not only what happened (the events), but also why it happened (interpretation) and the author's creativity (the style and form). The biblical authors were not just reporting events; they were seeking to explain the 'God-plot' (God at work in the world and in people's lives).

Biblical stories are stories with meaning and purpose, where beliefs take on flesh and blood in particular individuals and situations. In stories we see ourselves, or the people we would like to be, and a response is required of us. Our lives, too, are stories. Other people see our beliefs take on flesh and blood and witness our beliefs lived out in our lives. Stories are not something we just read, then analyse to find timeless truths; rather, we can live or 'indwell' a story, using it to understand our own experience. We can place our story alongside biblical stories to help us to make sense of our lives.

In *Reading the Bible Wisely*, Richard Briggs compares the original *Star Wars* experience of seeing the film on the big screen in the 1970s with the modern experience of watching the DVD in the front room. The big difference is that the first was an *involving* experience; the second was an *observing* experience. Anyone who has visited the Globe Theatre in London and stood in the pit may have found themselves suddenly to be part of the play and not just an observer. Briggs used the *Star Wars* analogy to illustrate that encountering biblical stories should be an involving experience.

Two brief examples will illustrate Briggs' point:

a. The Australian aboriginal experience is of dispossession from their land. In seeking to understand and interpret this experience the aboriginal community has embraced the story of Naboth's vineyard (1 Kings 21), where a powerful king robbed Naboth of his land. Naboth's story has become the aboriginal story, interpreting their experience, and enabling them to see that this sort of thing happens, even to good people, and that God cares about their plight.

b. The narrative of the Exodus is used by some black Christians as a means of understanding their community's experience of slavery and racism, allowing it to be interpreted positively in the light of God's liberation. Mark Sturge (2005) has explored this using an alternative Old Testament narrative – the stories of Joseph – in which the slave ceases to be a victim, rises above his troubles and is reconciled with his oppressors. This offers a different story to live by.

Reflection

How could the ways of viewing stories outlined in this section affect the way you use biblical stories in your ministry? Think of specific times when you use story and record your thoughts in your reflective diary.

Activity 4 (I): Finding your story, finding the God plot

a. Find a biblical story that echoes your experience in some way. Think about the following when choosing your story:

- ◆ in what ways can I legitimately claim this story as my own (in what ways does it echo my situation)?
- ◆ is the message of this story in line with the message of the whole Bible?
- ◆ is there any possibility that I might be abusing the biblical story in the way that I understand it?
- ◆ what positive effect on my attitudes and behaviour will living in the light of this story have?
- ◆ what are the dangers of living in the light of this story?
- ◆ how could the story be used in ministry?

b. Skim the story of Joseph (Genesis chapters 37 and 39–45) or Ruth or Esther. Note the 'God-Plot' of their lives. Record a brief account of your own life, or part of it, noting what happened and telling your story in any way you wish. For example, you can make a video diary or complete a life storyboard (see below). When you have finished your story, go over it and identify the God-plot in your life and note where *you perceived* God to be involved and moments when you thought God intervened. Think about how your story relates to the Bible story-line as a whole.

Activity 4 (G)

Follow the individual activities, but people may wish to do their storyboards/videos beforehand so that they have something to share with the group. Make it clear that the storyboard will be shared as that may determine what people write. Alternatively, storyboards can be done on the day.

Feedback

Here is part of my storyboard:

Mixed background, father hostile to Christianity, mother always prayerful. No interest in religion until mid teens. Concern about my own behaviour started me thinking.	Influence of cousin's quiet faith and discussion with another cousin. School assemblies led by the vicar and confirmation classes helped me to understand and accept the gospel, culminating in conversion at 17.	Very supportive church. Enormously helpful university CU. Meeting my future wife. Challenging experience of two years' National Service.
God working underground. Mother's prayers.	God made me unhappy, dissatisfied, open to hear him.	Strong awareness of God's presence and guidance.

5. Biblical genres and Christian ministry: using proverbs

Proverbs are memorable short sayings that capture an insight using homely images. They are often couched as opposites: wisdom and folly, love and hate (Proverbs 15:1, 16, 17). Proverbs can be found in the book of Proverbs and Ecclesiastes, but they are not restricted to these two books. A proverb is the result of a wise person looking at the world and being able to detect underlying trends, such as pride going before a fall. Some proverbs give advice on how to live: others are comments or observations. Proverbs give general principles to which there may be exceptions. Discernment is needed to know when a particular proverb applies and when it does not, particularly in pastoral situations. Proverbs are deceptively simple but their compacted wisdom can slowly be unpacked. This makes them useful pastorally as they are easy to grasp quickly, yet profound enough to increase in significance as a person reflects on them.

Reflection

Bearing in mind the nature of proverbs, how could you use them in your pastoral ministry? How could you capitalise on their simplicity and profundity? Record your thoughts in your reflective diary.

Activity 5 (I/G): Using Proverbs

Spend a few moments dipping into the book of Proverbs.

a. Locate a proverb that you think would be helpful in ministry.
b. Now find one that you think would be unhelpful.
c. Imagine the Book of Proverbs came with a label, 'Handle with care'. How would you explain this to someone beginning their pastoral ministry? What advice would you give on using proverbs in Christian ministry?

Feedback

a. Proverbs 25:1.
b. Proverbs 14:10 – unhelpful and depressing.
c. I would explain that proverbs are not advice to hand out like 'cure-all' tablets; both the proverb and the situation need careful thought. The pastor needs to ask if the proverb applies in this case. I like the idea that proverbs are the result of 'people-watching'. I would present them in this way and encourage others to observe life and decide if the proverb applied to that particular situation.

6. Biblical genres and Christian ministry: using parables

Jesus often communicated through parables. The term 'parable' is extremely broad and describes a certain type of vivid or unusual story that can be read at face value or at a much deeper level. The story describes a specific situation e.g. a woman losing a coin, but they can also stand for us all. The language of parables is symbolic and speaks to us directly, even if we cannot fully analyse the meaning. Parables force us to rethink, as we often find ourselves sympathising with the 'wrong' people, as in the labourers in the vineyard (Matthew 20:1–16). We sometimes have to unlearn previous attitudes. Here are three ways of seeing parables (there are more):

a. codes that people crack.

b. containers that carry meaning.

c. an art form that creates an encounter.

All of these ways of understanding parables can be useful, though which of the above three is appropriate will depend on the parable.

If we see parables as codes, we will start looking for what the different parts of the parable represent e.g. the different soils in the parable of the sower (Mark 4:1–9; 13–20).

If we think of parables as containers, we look at the similes involved and how they illuminate a point e.g. 'The Kingdom of God is like a mustard seed' (Mark 4:30–32).

If we see parables as an encounter then we will expect to be drawn into a relationship and often we will see ourselves depicted in the characters of these 'mini-stories' in some way. In some parables this comes as a shock as it did to King David in Nathan's parable (2 Samuel 12:1–13) when Nathan says, 'You are that man'. Parables use vivid images that sometimes jar: wayward boys who are forgiven and over-generous employers. Parables as encounters can shake us.

Activity 6 (I/G): Ways of understanding parables

Choose a parable and decide which of the three categorisations is appropriate to that parable. How could the different approaches to parables be used in your Christian ministry? Groups can work on this in pairs and share their results.

Feedback

I chose the parable of the unforgiving debtor (Matthew 18:23–34) and used the encounter model. I found myself identifying with the debtor (I usually identify with the indignant servants) and being challenged to live in gratitude when so much has been forgiven. I think using this approach with the emphasis on creating an encounter will be useful for preaching.

Final reflection

Think back over what you have done in this unit. What would your response be to the key question? Look again at your response to activity 3. Would you want to change anything in the light of this unit? What do you feel you would like to explore further? Record your thoughts in your reflective diary.

Review

As a result of studying this unit you should now be able to:

◆ articulate your understanding of the nature of the Bible and how it relates to Christian ministry.

◆ explain the implications of different genres for pastoral practice.

◆ give practical examples of how the Bible can shape the church and the wider community.

Resources

Ballard, P. and Holmes, S. R. (eds) (2005) *The Bible in Pastoral Practice*. Darton, Longman and Todd. Introduction and essay 11.

Bartholomew, C. G. and Goheen, M. W. (2004) *The Drama of Scripture: Finding Our Place in the Biblical Story*. Baker Academic.

Challis, W. (1997) *The Word of Life: Using the Bible in Pastoral Care*. Marshall Pickering.

Long, T. G. (1989) *Preaching the Literary Forms of the Bible*. Augsburg Fortress.

Lyall, D. (2001) *The Integrity of Pastoral Care* (New Library of Pastoral Care). SPCK. Chapter 5.

Oliver, G. (2006). *Holy Bible, Human Bible: Questions Pastoral Practice Must Ask*. Darton, Longman and Todd. Chapters 1–4.

Pattison, S. A. (2000) *Critique of Pastoral Care* (third edition). SCM. Chapter 6.

Peterson, E. H. (1980) *Five Smooth Stones for Pastoral Work*. Wm. B. Eerdmans Publishing Co.

Ryken, L. (1996) *Words of Delight: a Literary Introduction to the Bible* (second edition). Baker Book House.

Sturge, M. (2005) *Look What the Lord has Done: An Exploration of Black Christian Faith in Britain*. Scripture Union.

Wimberley, E. (1994) *Using Scripture in Pastoral Counseling*. Abingdon Press.

www.religion-online.org Select 'The Bible'

www.virtualrel.net Select 'Biblical studies'

www.findarticles.com Search by 'Bible genre' using free articles

www.ntgateway.com Search by 'Authority'

www.bibicalstudies.org.uk Select 'Bible', then 'Interpretation', then the genre you want

www.bible.gen.nz The post-modern Bible

Unit 3

What is my understanding of pastoral practice?

Key question
How does my understanding of what constitutes pastoral practice influence my use of the Bible in Christian ministry?

Preparation
You will need a local newspaper (page 41).

1. Introduction

You may be very clear concerning what you mean by pastoral practice, but in the literature definitions vary considerably. By spending time exploring what is meant by pastoral practice we can examine our own and other people's assumptions and review our ministry in the light of these.

Activity 1 (I): Imaging pastoral practice

Without thinking too much, write down any words and images that come into your mind when the term 'pastoral practice' is mentioned. Highlight words or images that you think are key ones. Using what you have written, sum up what pastoral practice means for you by writing a brief definition.

Activity 1 (G)

Use the activity for individuals, but write on a large sheet of paper. With a number of people contributing, you may notice the same or similar words occurring more than once. Highlight these as they may indicate where people agree. As a group, try to agree on a definition.

Feedback

Key words for me are 'care', 'involvement' and 'challenge'.
My definition: 'Helping people come to fullness of life based on God's truth'.

Reflection

Look at your definition and think about the following:

◆ Given your definition, should pastoral care be the province of those who are trained or should everyone be involved in some way in pastoring each other?

◆ Given your definition, what would the role of trained personnel be, e.g. clergy?

◆ Does your definition of pastoral care turn the church inwards upon itself or outwards towards the world?

2. Defining pastoral practice

It is perhaps easy and traditional to think of pastoral practice as being about the personal care of individuals and small groups, for example, at bereavement, weddings and when people have particular problems. However, many other kinds of activities may be pastoral or have a pastoral dimension. For example, preaching, teaching and visiting can all shape the way people develop and think about themselves. In all these activities, people can be helped to grow towards their God-given potential or away from it.

In this book we assume that pastoral practice is a very broad area which can embrace many different activities and contexts. It can take place in the church context or outside; it can be 'professional' or 'amateur', lay or clerical; it can include the nation, the community, the group and the individual. It is not only Christians who exercise pastoral care, but our concern here is with a definition of *Christian* pastoral practice/care. Stephen Pattison in *A Critique of Pastoral Care* suggests:

> *Pastoral care is that activity, undertaken especially by representative Christian persons, directed towards the elimination and relief of sin and sorrow and the presentation of all people perfect in Christ to God.*

This understanding gives pastoral care a positive goal as it aims for transformation: the presentation of all people perfect in Christ. Perfection is about wholeness and being complete. The definition is broad in that it encompasses both sin and sorrow, but it is not just problem-orientated. Pastoral care is for anyone, not just for Christians and it relates to society as well as to individuals, as sin and sorrow often have external causes. In this definition, both lay and clerical ministry are significant; pastoral ministry might be *especially* the responsibility of certain people within the church, but not *exclusively* so. Often the role of trained personnel will be to equip, enable and encourage others, and to act as a point around which others gather; a centre of standards, inspiration and training. For example, trained personnel can act as a standard for confidentiality and listening skills.

Although Stephen Pattison defines pastoral care as an *activity*, the *type* of people we are matters: it is not just what we do. No amount of good practice will ever be a substitute for the personal qualities of an individual. Having said this, many people find themselves taking on a pastoral role not because they are particularly gifted, not because they are trained, not even because they possess certain qualities, but because they happened to be there. Whatever the route, the church needs to recognise and support this wider ministry of pastoral care.

Activity 2 (I/G): Comparing definitions

Compare the definition/s you wrote in the first activity with Stephen Pattison's definition and decide if you want to make any changes. How far do you agree with Pattison's definition? How far do you disagree?

Feedback

I like Stephen Pattison's definition but I would put more of an emphasis on lay ministry and relate it more to using the Bible.

3. Different aspects of ministry

We have suggested that Christian ministry is broad and that most forms of ministry have a pastoral *dimension*. For example, worship is about giving glory to God but it also deals with issues of sin and sorrow (see Pattison's definition). More specifically, worship may be a springboard for growth and development, or it may crush people's spirits. This section is about thinking through the pastoral dimensions of your own particular ministry.

Look at the following five aspects that characterise pastoral care (identified by Clebsch, Jaekle and Clinebell). Each of these can reflect a biblically based idea, for example, the guiding of the Good Shepherd or Paul's nurturing of the young Christian communities.

   a. healing
   b. sustaining
   c. reconciling
   d. guiding
   e. nurturing

These different aspects will have varying prominence in different ministries; some will not feature at all in some contexts.

Activity 3 (I/G): The pastoral aspects of ministry

Write down one of the main Christian activities that form part of your ministry and, using the diagram, arrange the different aspects of pastoral care in the order of importance for that activity. Those near the top are more important. See the feedback for a worked example.

Feedback

My ministry in the Church is largely with young children and involves me primarily in sustaining, guiding and nurturing them.

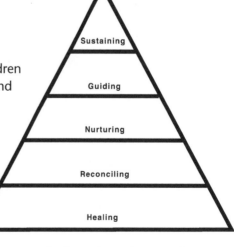

Reflection

It is not only within churches that pastoral ministry is exercised. Pastoral ministry is often exercised outside the church within secular spheres and in doing so becomes part of the church's mission. Many activities have pastoral dimensions that can be recognised and celebrated by the Church. Think about people in your church whose work or daily life involves them in pastoral ministry in some way. What recognition do these people receive for the work that they do? How could your church celebrate their ministry? How could you make them feel that they are acting as representatives of the church in this secular ministry? Record your thoughts in your reflective diary.

4. The wider situation

Pastoral practice is often personal and individually focused, but can it also be political and social? The individual may be one focus of pastoral practice, but if the individual remains the *only* concern it can become a mopping up exercise that does not address the causes of sin and sorrow. This means that sometimes social, economic and political problems have to be addressed if pastoral care is to be effective. As Martin Luther King pointed out, we cannot keep being Good Samaritans; in the end we have to do something about the robbers on the road. That does not mean we cease to act in individual cases when we can't immediately change the situation. We cannot wait for a perfect world before we minister, but neither can we ignore the situations that create the pastoral problems.

Widening the scope of pastoral practice to the social and political reflects what often happened in the Bible: Moses, Joseph, Daniel and Esther all engaged with issues at a political level. Prophets such as Isaiah comforted and challenged whole nations. It could even be argued that the pastoral witness of the Bible is mainly oriented towards the organisation and nurturing of communities, even nations, not primarily towards individuals. In this respect the Bible might challenge us to think more broadly about the very nature of pastoral care and practice. Shepherds in the Bible were leaders of groups of people or sheep, not individual counsellors.

When the local TV news started, Gareth watched with growing horror. He had been a visitor at the local care home for the elderly for years. He had visited regularly and brought a team from his church to run services. He had even organised teas at church and had a rota of church members who collected people from the care home and took them back. He had never noticed any abuse and none of the residents had ever complained to him. He had noticed how quiet and subdued they were but he had thought this to be one of the signs of ageing. Now the headlines were of scandalous abuse of the elderly involving bullying and the misuse of medication at this very establishment. Gareth was asking himself if he had missed the point in his ministry by simply focusing on the residents and not their wider situation.

Activity 4 (I): Beyond the individual

Looking at the case study, what could and should Gareth have done?

Activity 4 (G)

Role-play Gareth being questioned on a local radio phone in, what questions might be asked? What might be his response?

Reflection

Think of one person with whom you have been involved pastorally and reflect on their situation (keep it anonymous). How did the social, spiritual, political, economic and other factors relate in this case? Record your thoughts in your reflective diary.

Feedback

Although in many ways Gareth was not in a position to influence the care home he could have widened his ministry to include the staff. That might have alerted him to the problems sooner. This one change could have given him a very different perspective. Once aware of the problem he could have acted on the residents' behalf.

5. A corporate effort

The church on the Greenall estate saw itself as a local church, serving its own area. The church pastoral team was keen to reach out to the community, but the scale of the need was enormous and they knew they would not be able to cope. Sharing the problem with the congregation, it was decided to hold a series of sessions on reaching out to friends and neighbours. During the meetings the pastoral team discovered that a lot was already going on informally that had not been recognised, so a strategy was developed that incorporated this activity but also offered training and opened up other possibilities.

Most people shy away from widening the scope of pastoral practice, not only because they fear losing its personal focus, but from fear of being swamped with work – focusing on the individual keeps the job under control! The Christian tradition generally supports the notion that it is the whole body of Christ that exercises God's ministry in the world, not *just* individual Christians (though affirming this wider ministry in no way denies the more formal role of 'pastor'). The research project showed evidence of ministry being increasingly shared, either in a team ministry situation or by people informally getting together. Ministry can be widened further, with pastors encouraging people to act pastorally where they are, in the church and in the community. This involves a different model of pastoral care where trained personnel become enablers as in the case study.

Activity 5 (I/G): Working with others

What do you think might be the advantages and disadvantages of people involved in pastoral practice working together? Jot down brief notes.

Feedback

Advantages: more energy, fuller interpretations, more ideas, accountability to a group, discernment, support, supervision of action.

Disadvantages: group norms may hold back individual concern, getting together may be difficult, etc.

6. Working together in the wider community

Churches can play important roles in their local community. For examples of work in the local community go to www.faithworks.info. More examples can be found on the *Fresh Expressions* DVD (www.freshexpressions.org.uk).

... AND PLEASE WELCOME OUR NEW MEMBERS, A COUPLE OF WHOM COME FROM OUR VERY OWN LOCAL CHURCH.....

Working in the community as part of the wider pastoral ministry of the church needs careful thought. Here are some pointers for action: others can be found in *Changing Communities* on which this section draws (see the resource section).

◆ Get to know the communities better and find out about local concerns and issues. Those who live and work in the community help to build the picture.

◆ Analyse the situation so that the underlying issues and what needs to change are understood. Serious thought and prayer needs to given to what the Bible has to say to the situation.

For convenience's sake I have split these two processes, but in practice they are inter-woven.

a. Analysing the situation and initiating change

◆ Listen carefully, and then describe the issue.

◆ What is already being done? Who is doing it?

◆ Map the people who are involved e.g. government departments, local charities and people in the community who are affected by it.

◆ Who has the power in this situation? Who makes the decisions? Who benefits? Who loses?

◆ What has to be changed to put this situation right? Can this be broken down into steps? Challenges can look less scary when approached one step at a time.

◆ What are our gifts? What do we bring to this situation?

◆ Who can we work with? We don't have to do everything ourselves.

◆ Initiate action but take time to reflect prayerfully on it: it's not a case of starting something and just letting it roll without reviewing it.

◆ Celebrate change.

b. Bringing biblical insights

We could:

◆ bring the questions that arise from the community situation to the Bible, rather than read the text then try to apply it to daily life (pages 54–61).
◆ ask: 'Is this a subject about which the Bible has something specific to say?'
◆ ask if the biblical narrative (the big story of fall and redemption) has anything to say to this situation.
◆ look for biblical principles or ways of thinking that are relevant. For example, a biblical worldview includes the idea that this world is not perfect. We should do as much as we can to alleviate suffering and combat evil but we will never be able to create a utopia in this life. This has to be born in mind, for solutions that depend on an over-optimistic view of humanity will not work.
◆ allow the Bible to be radical. What might it be saying about *our* lifestyles and ways of thinking? Are we part of the solution or part of the problem?
◆ ask what the Bible has to say to the whole community, not just to individuals.

Some things to bear in mind

Change involves churches being part of the community, not sanctuaries where people escape from it. It entails getting involved in community life. Small grassroots communities can be very effective – big is not always best. 'Glocalisation' is the strengthening of local communities, returning power to them and involving them in positive change, rather than imposing change or doing it for them.

Activity 6 (I/G): Getting involved

Using a local newspaper or your knowledge of the area, identify an issue for your community that also impacts on your Christian ministry.

a. Use some of the tools from the two lists to begin to explore it (you may not have time to use them all).
b. Which part of the process do you think you will find most difficult?
c. Can you think of a way of overcoming it?

Feedback

I only had time to look at a few tools from each list.

a. We identified the issue of the distance of hospitals from our community. They are so far away that visitors find it difficult to get there, which means that clergy and church members often get involved in transport and other visiting arrangements. We located a group of GPs who were already thinking about this. They want to take over a closed 'cottage hospital' and reopen it as a recovery centre where patients could come once they no longer needed specialised hospital care. The church could work with this group.
b. I think the part I will find most difficult will be relating biblical passages to the situation or seeing if the whole biblical story has anything to say.
c. I think our group might ask for a member of the clergy to help with the use of biblical insights.

Final reflection

Go back to the key question: how would you answer it? Look back at your definition of pastoral practice. Has anything made you reconsider the way you think about pastoral practice? Has anything confirmed what you already do? Record your thoughts in your reflective diary.

Review

As a result of studying this unit you should now be able to:

◆ articulate your understanding of pastoral practice and its aims
◆ explain the different pastoral aspects of Christian ministry
◆ describe ways of people working together in the community as part of their wider Christian ministry and the role of the Bible might play in this.

Resources

Atkinson, D. and Field, D. (eds) (1995) *New Dictionary of Christian Ethics and Pastoral Theology.* Inter-varsity Press.

Ballard, P. and Pritchard, J. (2006) *Practical Theology in Action: Christian Thinking in the Service of Church and Society* (revised edition). SPCK.

Carr, W. (ed.) (2002) *The New Dictionary of Pastoral Studies.* SPCK.

Goodliff, P. (1998) *Care in a Confused Climate.* Darton, Longman and Todd.

Hinton, J. and Price, P. B. (2003) *Changing Communities: Church from the Grass Roots.* Churches Together in Britain and Ireland.

Hunter, R. (ed.), (1990) *Dictionary of Pastoral Care and Counseling.* Abingdon Press.

Lyall, D. (2001) *The Integrity of Pastoral Care* (New Library of Pastoral Care). SPCK. Chapter 7.

Pattison, S. (2000) *A Critique of Pastoral Care* (third edition). SCM. Chapters 1 and 5.

Pattison, S. (1994) *Pastoral Care and Liberation Theology.* Cambridge University Press.

Tidball, D. (1986) *Skilful Shepherds.* Inter-varsity Press.

Woodward, J. and Pattison. S. (eds) (2000) *The Blackwell Reader in Pastoral and Practical Theology.* Blackwell Publishing Ltd. Chapter 11.

www.acc.uk.org Select 'Pastoral care' and 'Ethics and practice'
www.religion-online.org Select 'Practical theology' and 'Church and society'
www.findarticles.com Search by 'Pastoral care' using free articles
www.pastoralreport.com go to 'Links' for a range of sites

Section 2

The Issues

Unit 4
The authority of the Bible

Key question:
How does my understanding of the authority of the Bible affect the way I use it in Christian ministry?

1. Introduction

All Christian traditions regard the Bible as an authority, but how this authority is viewed varies. The research project revealed a range of opinions and an equally broad range of approaches in pastoral practice, but there was no *simple* equation between the view of Scripture held and the way the Bible was used. Our instinctive feelings about the idea of authority seem to be influenced by a number of factors, e.g. our general approach to life, our personality and the tradition to which we belong.

This unit explores this range of views so that you can clarify how you think the Bible acts as an authority and what difference that makes in Christian ministry. This is a controversial topic and you may find studying the variety of views challenging. But the fact is that Christians do disagree and it is important to understand why we differ and how this leads to different practice in Christian ministry. If you begin to feel uncomfortable, or angry, that is to be expected; don't be put off, because the important thing is that you understand more clearly what you think about the authority of the Bible and how that will influence your Christian ministry. You are not being asked to change your theological position, but you are being asked to reflect on your position and how it affects your practice. Of course the authors have their own views and you might be able to spot them as you work through the unit, but this is not intended to be prescriptive.

Activity 1 (I): Exploring authority as a concept

What does the word 'authority' conjure up in your mind?

a. Draw some scales on a piece of paper. Label one side 'positive' and another 'negative' (see feedback).
b. On a piece of paper, write down in two minutes as many words as you can think of in response to the word 'authority'. Don't think hard about this; just write words as they come into your head.
c. Then sort them into words with positive associations and words with negative associations by writing them on the appropriate sides of the scales.

Activity 1 (G)

Use the activity for individuals, but write the words on scraps of paper or post-it notes. Draw the scales on a large sheet of paper, or use two circles made from string, label them 'positive' and 'negative' and place them on the floor/table. Group members put their words in the appropriate place on the scales or in the appropriate circle.

Activity 1 (I/G)

What does the previous activity tell you about your general attitude to the concept of authority? How might this affect your attitude to the idea of the Bible being an authority? If you think of your reactions to the idea of authority of the Bible as being similar to a reading on a thermometer, with 100°C being very positive and 0°C being very negative, where would you fall on the scale? Mark the thermometer.

Feedback

This is my list of positive and negative factors concerning authority. I would mark my thermometer at about 70°C, which is surprising as my attitude to the Bible is more positive than my attitude to authority and the establishment in general.

Positive	**Negative**
Law and order	Nepotism
Power	Dictatorship
Influence	Corruption
	Power

2. Facing the challenge of using the Bible

There are times when we yearn for authoritative answers without the hard work of interpreting the Bible. This case study is an illustration of this.

A member of your church has been searching the internet to purchase a Bible. He has found a version called God's Word. *The strap line is:* Today's Bible translation that says what it means. *The accompanying blurb claims that no interpretation is needed in reading this Bible and that this translation allows you to immediately understand exactly what the original writers meant. He is very excited about this as he finds many Bible translations obscure and difficult to apply. He wants to buy this version because he thinks it will give him clear instructions as to how to live his life.*

Reflection

Imagine emailing this person with a comment on their reaction to this Bible translation.

◆ What would you say?
◆ To what degree do you think the Bible gives authoritative, clear cut teaching like this? Can you give any examples?
◆ How much do you think your reaction to this case study was influenced by your

underlying feelings about the concept of authority in general? Record your thoughts in your reflective diary.

Note: the issue of interpretation is dealt with in unit 5.

3. Three views of the authority of the Bible

In this section we will review three different views on how the Bible acts as an authority (remembering that all such simple classifications are always in need of qualification). These are described briefly below, together with an illustrative case study for each.

a. The Bible as a blueprint and pattern

In this view the Bible, as God's Word, is seen as the absolute authority in relation to Christian belief and life. The job of the Christian is to apply its clear and timeless teaching in everyday life.

> *Phil and Ruth believed that the Bible gave them a pattern for living. Both had a ministry within the church but both believed that that men and women served God in different ways with leadership being the responsibility of men. The Bible also set the pattern for family life, with a strong emphasis on home and family for them both but with a particular nurturing role for Ruth. They were fortunate enough not to be so pressurised financially that she had to work outside the home.*

The basic attitude towards the Bible is one of great respect and the response is obedience. The meaning of the Bible is usually regarded as being unambiguous and fixed. The Bible is believed to reveal the absolute will of God and is assumed to relate *directly* to modern life.

b. The Bible as model and guide

In this view the Bible is still the prime authority and has a revered place as the Word of God, but it is only properly understood through careful study by Christians in community. It offers many *paradigms* (models) for how God deals with the human race, but rarely acts as a *blueprint* that can be applied without further thought. The meaning is not *always* straightforward and the text does not *necessarily* provide *specific* instructions on how to live today. The goal is to achieve *dynamic equivalence* between the meaning of the text in its original context and its implementation in the world today as illustrated in the case study.

> *Gemma's housegroup read Acts 2:44–46 as part of their study and wondered if this still applied today. Should they really be giving up their possessions and living communally? They invited the minister to talk through the issue and together they worked out what the dynamic equivalent action might be today. They identified ways of strengthening the bond between members so that they could live more communally in the modern world. They began a scheme for sharing some equipment in order to free money to share with those in need, which then expanded into a skills sharing scheme.*

The basic attitude towards the Bible is one of ultimate respect and trust, but with recognition of the need to work at understanding the meaning for today. Before this authority the person stands with humility, accepting their own fallibility in interpreting the text (unit 5). In the final analysis, the Christian's responsibility is to follow authoritative biblical teachings by living out the dynamic equivalent meanings.

c. The Bible as inspiration

In this view the Bible is seen as inspiring literature akin to other great literary works. The authority of the Bible relates to its having been identified by the historic Church as having particular value. It retains authority because Christian communities continue to treat it with reverence and respect. It is, however, a human work and its authority lies in its ability generally to inspire, question and inform, not because it reveals the will of God in a direct and special way.

> *In the debate about the gay lifestyle, some Christians are taking the view that those who quote Paul and Leviticus in condemnation of homosexuality are forgetting that their views developed in a context where the evils of discrimination were not recognised. Thus slavery was not contested. The Church should update its teaching in the light of the new knowledge. To do so is to be truly biblical because this reflects the overall teaching that humans are all made in the image of God. Paul and the author of Leviticus do not have the authority to decide the issue for modern people.*

The basic attitude to the Bible is one of respect, but tinged with considerable suspicion because of the danger of allowing it to do the thinking for us which we should be doing it for ourselves.

Activity 3 (I/G): Biblical authority and Christian ministry

Individuals should jot down notes in response to these activities. Groups should allow individuals or pairs time to generate responses and then should listen to each others' reflections without passing comment.

a. Think of two or three Christians in your past who have had a significant influence on you. Can you identify which view of biblical authority they each held? How was this revealed, if at all? Did it make a significant difference to their ministry with you? Does reflecting on the influence of these people on you offer any insights as to how you think your view of biblical authority might influence your own ministry?

b. Imagine that you have a child in their late teens who has come under the influence of a Christian who holds a very different view of the authority of the Bible from your own. You want to write to your child expressing your views about this influence. Make some bullet point notes on the things that you might write.

c. Identify two contemporary pastoral questions from the media. Possible examples include: Should gay partnerships be officially recognised? Should individuals be encouraged to save for their retirement before they give to good causes? Create a table (see the feedback) and jot some notes in it to indicate briefly how people holding each of these approaches to biblical authority might handle these pastoral questions.

Feedback

a. I was influenced by a teacher who was, I think, liberal in his view of biblical authority but this didn't change my own evangelical faith. I had enormous respect for him and took his opinions seriously. He taught me to think critically about the Bible.

I also feel greatly indebted to my Open Brethren background even though I reacted against some of the narrowness I experienced there. I was very influenced by the respect for Scripture even if I did not agree with the view of the authority many people in the congregation held.

b. Bullet points to son/daughter:

◆ How comfortable and at ease are you in church?
◆ Will the leadership talk to parents/friends?
◆ How does this church talk about people who hold a different view?

c. I identified cohabitation and women bishops as current issues.

Question	Bible as blueprint	Bible as model and guide	Bible as inspiration
Should the church always oppose cohabitation?	I think they would say 'Yes' but this position is harder than might be thought to support by direct biblical references.	I think they would pose questions about the significance of marriage as the basis of relationships. They would put the emphasis on faithfulness and responsibility.	I think they would accept a relationship, or a series of relationships in the light of modern society. They would stress the responsible use of contraception.
Should women be consecrated as bishops?	Many would argue against female leadership at any level, claiming biblical warranty but ignoring examples of women leaders in the OT and NT.	I think they would take seriously the place of women in the gospels and the epistles and relate it to the changed social situation of woman in modern western society.	I think they would argue for women bishops but would not seek biblical warranty.

4. Strengths, weakness and consistency

Each position on the authority of the Bible has its strengths and weaknesses; there is no such thing as a 'problem-free' position. The South American theologian Rubem Alves has suggested that everyone is liberal in some respects and literalistic in other respects. For example so-called liberal Christians can be very literalistic when it comes to teaching on social morality (e.g. on wealth), but very liberal when it comes to biblical teaching on personal morality.

Reflection

Do you agree with Rubem Alves? What might cause such inconsistency? Do you think that Christians are as consistent over biblical authority as they sometimes claim to be? Think about your own view of biblical authority: how consistent are you? Record your thoughts in your reflective diary.

Activity 4 (I): Evaluating different views of biblical authority

List the strengths and weaknesses of each approach using a table (see the feedback).

Activity 4 (G)

Write the three different views on large sheets of paper, leaving plenty of room for people to write notes and comments. Place them in different parts of the room. Each member of the group will need a pen and should walk around and add comments on the strengths and weaknesses of the relevant position to each piece of paper. After three or four minutes, the group should divide into three sub-groups. Each takes one sheet of paper and prepares a presentation for the rest of the group on the strengths and weaknesses of the position on their sheet of paper. Finally the group should discuss their responses to the activity.

Feedback

My view on the strengths and weaknesses is:

	Strengths	Weaknesses
Bible as blueprint	Certainty, simplicity.	Can appear as dogmatic and narrow.
Bible as model and guide	Thoughtful, dynamic relationship between the Bible and now.	Loss of clarity. Can lapse into syncretism.
Bible as inspiration	Freedom from outdated constraints. Ability to move on.	No anchors. No source of objective guidance. Too subjective.

Reflection

Which of these three views is closest to your own? Do you ever feel under any pressure to adopt a different view in your pastoral ministry? If so, where is this pressure coming from and why? Think of an example from pastoral practice where you have been aware that you and another person were working with different views of the authority of the Bible. For example, does a person's view of the authority of the Bible affect their leadership style? (Leadership styles can have far-reaching pastoral effects.) Record your thoughts in your reflective diary.

5. The authority of a narrative

One emerging influence on understanding of how the Bible acts as an authority for contemporary Christians is narrative theology. This approach regards story as the primary genre in the Bible. All the other genres, e.g. commands, epistles, laws, poetry, are commentary on the narratives of God's dealings with humans through history. Tom Wright developed a now famous analogy where he compared the Bible to the completion of an unfinished Shakespeare play. In it, Wright is attempting to explain what it means to live in the light of the authority of the biblical text. A modified version of his analogy is given below:

> *Imagine that we have discovered a previously unknown Shakespeare play, which had seven acts, but with the sixth missing. How would we go about completing the play so it could be performed? The answer is to employ several experienced Shakespearean actors and ask them to write and stage the missing sixth act, taking into account the plot, characters and themes of the unfinished play and their own knowledge of Shakespeare. What would the result be? Undoubtedly there would be as many different plays as there are actors involved. But we would expect each of their scripts to be clearly and recognisably a legitimate sixth act for this play; the sort of thing that Shakespeare himself might have written. The best sixth act would be that which was creative, but also clearly developed under the authority of Shakespeare's original work, thereby being the most authentic completion.*

This analogy is meant to explain how the Bible can act as an authority for life now. Acts I-V of the play can be understood as the five scenes from the Bible's story of creation, the fall into sin, the story of Israel, the story of Jesus Christ and the story of the Church. Act VII is the final consummation of salvation history. Act VI is the period between the early church and the final consummation; the period in which we now live. In order to 'write' the sixth act, we have to live out a creative but authentic interpretation of acts I-V and VII.

The analogy juggles the ideas of freedom and constraint, authority and creativity. Creativity is encouraged in applying the Bible to modern life and thereby implies that it is rarely ever true that there is only *one way* of being biblical. There is also constraint in emphasising that the authority of the Bible controls the possible applications that can be made (i.e. by matching the previous acts in the play). The analogy is intended to help understand what it might mean to live under the authority of the biblical text in the modern world.

Activity 5 (I/G): Evaluating the analogy

a. How helpful might the analogy be for living in the modern world? What freedom and creativity does it allow in practice? What constraints and authority does it impose?
b. What difference could it make in pastoral situations?

Feedback

a. I found the Shakespeare analogy very helpful. For one thing it helped me to realise that living under the authority of the Bible needn't be a rigid affair. I can be creative in the way I apply it in my own life, yet there is still guidance and authority since I am not free to interpret the Bible in any way I like.
b. This could give me greater freedom in pastoral situations. Instead of trying to find *the* authoritative verse for a particular pastoral situation, I will encourage people to be both creative and faithful to Scripture by writing their own 'sixth act'.

Final reflection

Read the key question again and consider your response in light of your study so far. What in this unit have you found the most challenging? What has been most helpful? Record your thoughts in your reflective diary.

Review

As a result of studying this unit you should now be able to:

◆ explain a range of views concerning the authority of the Bible and how they influence pastoral practice.
◆ articulate your own understanding of the authority of the Bible and its influence on your ministry.
◆ describe how biblical narrative can act as an authority for living in day-to-day situations.

Assess the degree to which you think you have achieved each of these.

Resources

Ballard, P. and Holmes, S. R. (eds) (2005) *The Bible in Pastoral Practice.* Darton, Longman and Todd. Part II.

Briggs, R. (2003) *Reading the Bible Wisely.* Baker Academic.

Borg, M. (2001) *Reading the Bible Again for the First Time.* HarperCollins.

Kraft, C. H. 'The Church in Culture: A Dynamic Equivalence Model' in *Down to Earth: Studies in Christianity and Culture: The Papers of the Lausanne Consultation on Gospel and Culture*, Coote, R. T. and Stott, J. (eds) (1980). Hodder & Stoughton.

Oliver, G. (2006) *Holy Bible, Human Bible: Questions Pastoral Practice Must Ask.* Darton, Longman and Todd. Chapter 7.

Smith, D. and Shortt, J. (2002) *The Bible and the Task of Teaching.* The Stapleford Centre.

Wright, C. (1991). 'The Authority of Scripture in an Age of Relativism' in *The Gospel in the Modern World*, Eden, M. and Wells, D. (eds). Inter-Varsity Press.

Wright, T. (1993). *The New Testament and the People of God.* SPCK. See especially pages 139–43.

www.bibicalstudies.org.uk Select 'Bible' then 'Interpretation' then 'Authority'

www.religion-online.org Select 'Authority of the Bible'

www.virtualrel.net Select 'Christianity' then 'Scriptures'

www.findarticles.com Search by 'Bible authority' using free articles

www.users.ox.ac.uk/ctitext2/theology/ A comprehensive list of sites for theology on the web.

www.safeinchurch.co.uk

Unit 5

Applying the Bible in the contemporary context

Key question
How can the Bible be applied in contemporary situations of Christian ministry?

1. Introduction

Applying the Bible to everyday living is a challenge for any Christian; in the twenty-first century it sometimes seems harder than ever, as the culture in which we live becomes more and more distant from the world of the Bible. The people who wrote the Bible inhabited a very different historical and cultural context from pastoral practitioners today. Given that, it is important to examine how we interpret and apply the Bible in our increasingly complex, plural and global situation. In the research project, practitioners of differing theological stances recognised the challenge and were anxious not to dump ancient texts on modern society without explanation and interpretation. However, the pressures of Christian ministry often mean that this aspiration is abandoned for a more pragmatic approach.

Reflection

Think back through your own experience of applying the Bible, either in your own life or in your pastoral ministry. Identify an example of:

a. a situation where you found it easy to apply the Bible.
b. a situation where you found it was not straightforward to apply the Bible.

Reflect on what made the difference. To what degree was the difference in cultural context between the Bible and the situation a factor? Record your thoughts in your reflective diary.

2. The process of interpretation and application

In the process of interpreting and applying the Bible there are three main factors to consider:

♦ the Bible;
♦ the culture, assumptions and beliefs of the person applying it;
♦ the nature of the particular contemporary situation in which it is being applied.

The interaction between these three factors, and which factor is emphasised, varies from person to person. It also differs across traditions and contexts. Read the three case studies below; in each, consider the relative influence of the three factors and how they are interacting. Which factor is being emphasised most? How does it impact on the other two?

Ellie

My training in biblical studies is the foundation for my pastoral ministry; it is to this that I turn first when preparing for preaching, teaching and other pastoral work. I then ask God to lay on my heart those timeless biblical truths that I need to apply in any particular situation.

Grace

Before I trained for Christian ministry, I worked as a social worker. I found that basic sociology and psychology gave me important insights into the human situation. As a matter of principle in pastoral situations, I turn first to these disciplines so that I have a clear understanding of the issues and practices involved before I look to the Bible for passages that will support these insights.

Simeon

I start by saying to myself, 'what are the really important questions that people face in this particular situation?' I then go to the Bible for insights in dealing with those questions. I think that being biblical doesn't simply mean imitating the way things were done in biblical times. Rather it means asking important questions about how we live now and how the Bible relates to these.

Activity 2 (I): Evaluating the influence of the three factors

a. Create a diagram for each case study that illustrates the importance given to each of the factors by the people involved (see feedback). Use the diagram to illustrate how they each think the three factors are interacting with each other.

Having drawn your three diagrams, jot down a sentence or two in response to the following questions:

b. Which case study is closest to your own practice? What does that indicate as to the most important principle that *you* think applies in using the Bible in Christian ministry?

c. What are the strengths of the other two approaches that you need to keep in mind as helpful balances to your own approach?

Activity 2 (G)

Create diagrams as a group on flip chart paper and use questions b. and c. for group discussion.

Feedback

a. My diagrams:

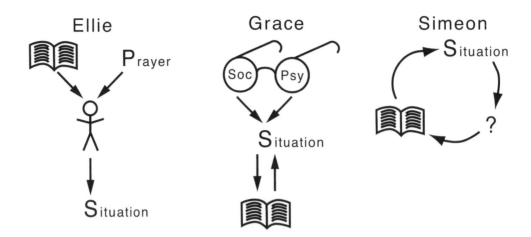

b. I am closest to Simeon because I think that understanding the questions that people are asking in today's world is important. I have met too many people who say 'Here are the answers, oh and by the way, what was the question you wanted to ask?'

c. I think I have to listen carefully to Ellie because it is easy for me to focus too much on today's concerns and not to allow myself to be challenged by biblical ideas. I also need to listen to Grace because she is highlighting the importance of knowing what your own concerns and interests are. If I am not aware of them I might easily just take them for granted and let them over-influence my reading of the Bible.

3. Biblical interpretation and application as a conversation

Stephen Pattison (2000) describes pastoral practice as a conversation, between the Bible, the person and the situation. He uses the metaphor of a conversation because he wants to convey the idea of a dialogue. It communicates the idea of a living, mutually respectful, and attentive process that evolves and changes rather than the idea that fixed truths are deposited into modern situations. It reflects the well-known model of the pastoral cycle (unit 9 section 3) where the interplay between human experience and the biblical text is fundamental to the pastoral process. (See http://www.neafe.org/docs/saltley/pastoralcycle.pdf. for a diagram of the pastoral cycle.)

The conversation metaphor doesn't pre-determine the relative significance of each partner. For some people the Bible will be the primary voice, whereas for others it will be the needs of the situation or the human voice of the person applying the Bible. This issue of the relative authority of the partners is covered in unit 4.

For the rest of this unit we are going to develop the conversation model as a case study. Here we will focus on the second and third conversation partners, the person and the situation. We will not look at the Bible as the important issues relating to its role as a conversation partner are covered elsewhere in the book. They include understanding the original context, establishing the genre and discerning the theological intentions of the author.

The conversation metaphor is an influential model and it is therefore important to understand it. However, you do not have to agree with it, so as you work through the rest of this unit keep asking yourself how convincing and helpful you find it.

Reflection

Think about the metaphor of conversation. What advantages does it have in helping us to think about applying the Bible? Do you think it has any disadvantages? Taking the situation that you described earlier where you found it difficult to apply the Bible, would thinking about the process in this way have helped at all? Record your thoughts in your reflective diary.

4. The person: the second conversation partner

As humans we are all prone to reading the biblical texts in ways that make us feel comfortable. Read the case study below.

The Dutch Reformed Church of the apartheid era of South African history taught that the Bible supported a political structure that favoured separate development of the races and the superiority of the Afrikaner. This was based on the belief that Afrikaners were a special people who, like the Israelites, were given the land by God and were to keep themselves pure and not mix with the 'Canaanites'. For many at that time, this doctrine was an unquestioned assumption and pastoral thinking was shaped by that assumption. However in 1986, the leaders of the Church officially repented, declaring apartheid to be a sin because it contravened the biblical teaching of neighbourly love. These leaders came to recognise that they had colluded in using the Bible to further their own interests against the interest of others.

The South African example is an extreme one. But it illustrates how Christians were unable to see that their political assumptions were distorting their interpretation and application of the Bible. They were reading the Bible through a particular set of lenses provided by their background, their experience of life and their concern for their own community. This meant they thought they found apartheid in its pages. Their thinking was eventually challenged by becoming more open to the questions raised by other Christians and through incidents that led to an increasing sense of shame. This is an example of how a conversation between the Bible, the person and the situation can lead to new understanding and revised pastoral practice.

Gordon Oliver (2006) has introduced the idea that the Bible is to be viewed as a stranger in our midst from whom we can learn. His metaphor challenges an attitude of mind that treats the Bible as 'familiar friend', where we converse with it in such a way that we expect agreement. We certainly don't expect it to challenge our basic assumptions about the Christian life. However, in biblical terms, that is just what the stranger will do. In our welcoming of him, there is also the expectation that we are going to be challenged, possibly even experience a culture shock that will shake us to the core. We might call this experience 'Bible shock'.

Activity 4 (I): Can the Bible shock?

a. Identify a situation or occasion when you have experienced Bible shock. It doesn't matter if it is something quite trivial. The important point is that you can identify the experience that goes with the loss of a taken-for-granted assumption 'about how things are'. Write a brief (maximum 50 words) summary of the incident.

b. Now try and identify a group of Christians who you think *ought* to experience Bible shock. What is it about their basic assumptions that you regard as highly questionable? How does this lead them to behave pastorally in ways you regard as unfaithful to biblical teaching? Again, write a brief summary.

c. Now for the hard part! Imagine a Christian who holds different views from you; it may be a Christian from another country, culture or denomination. Imagine them coming to a Bible study in your home. What assumptions that you automatically make might they challenge? Now imagine the Bible is this stranger who joins your group. What might cause your group Bible shock? Write an imaginary diary entry for the Bible study recording how your visitor helped you to realise that you were reading the Bible through a particular set of lenses that needed challenging.

Activity 4 (G)

Use the individual activity as the basis for group discussion. It is however recommended that activity b. be undertaken as a silent reflection where each group member thinks of their own example. Otherwise the session could become unhelpfully negative towards others. Other ideas for developing the group activity are:

◆ With activity a. ask group members to work in pairs so that everyone has a good chance to share their experience.

◆ With activity c. either the whole group can focus on one 'stranger' and discuss in detail how he/she would challenge the group. (A variation would be for one member of the group to role-play being the stranger.) Or each member of the group can share their thoughts on who their 'stranger' would be and how they would be the bringer of Bible shock.

Feedback

a. For me such a shock came when I met some Japanese Christians. They were puzzled by my attitude to authority and pointed out that I was blind to the place given to authority, particularly of parents, in the biblical text. As child of the 1960s, I had imported the general disregard for authority characteristic of my generation into the Bible without realising it.

b. I think that Christians who preach that illness and poverty are the result of a lack of faith or sin ought to experience Bible shock.

c. Marta, a member of a church group visiting from Kenya, joined our Bible study group. Her story challenged our western individualism and in the light of her visit we began to look again at some of St Paul's teaching.

5. The situation: the third conversation partner

In order to apply the Bible today we need to think very carefully about how we transfer its teaching from one culture or situation to another in an appropriate way. The following quotation comes from a Sri Lankan theologian, Dr D. T. Niles:

> *The gospel is like a seed and you have to sow it. When you sow the*
> *seed of Christianity in Palestine, a plant that can be called*

Palestinian Christianity grows. When you sow it in Rome, a plant called Roman Christianity grows. You sow the gospel in Great Britain and you get British Christianity. Now, when the missionaries came to our lands they brought not only the seed of the gospel, but also their own plant of Christianity, flowerpot included! So what we have to do is to break the flowerpot, take out the seed of the gospel, sow it in our own cultural soil, and let our version of Christianity grow.

Activity 5a (I/G): Evaluating Dr Niles' analogy

This may be the first time you have encountered this analogy. If not, imagine that it is. Jot down up to six bullet points to send in an email to Dr Niles telling him what was helpful and what worried you about his analogy.

Feedback

Dear Dr Niles,
I thought your seed analogy was great because:

◆ it made me realise how much of my Christian faith comes from my culture.
◆ it made me think about what were the essentials of the faith (the seed).
◆ it brought home how easy it is to impose my particular way of being Christian on other people (e.g. our patterns of worship).

However I wasn't sure that the analogy didn't confuse things because:

◆ it seems to imply that there is a 'seed' that is completely independent of culture. But are not all expressions of Christianity culturally bound?

Niles' analogy highlights the importance of understanding the situation in which we hope to 'sow' biblical insights. Each new pastoral encounter needs to be approached with the same care as a new culture. The challenge in applying the Bible to a pastoral situation is to understand that situation enough to avoid dumping on other people our own perception of biblical ideas based on our own situation and experience of life. Stephen Pattison has called this mistake 'situational fundamentalism', which he defines as: 'because something is true in one's own experience, it must be true for all people everywhere' (2000, p143).

When Gentiles started to become Christians in large numbers, new questions and issues were raised as they came from very different backgrounds to Jews. Should they be circumcised? Could they eat meat sacrificed to idols? The Early Church had to respond to this new pastoral situation in ways that were appropriate for the Gentile Christians. The Acts of the Apostles and the Epistles record the differences of opinion that resulted. Pastoral practitioners today are having similarly to respond to uncharted situations, so don't expect this to be an easy task!

Niles' approach reflects an idea commonly called contextualisation or incultura-tion, which is now widely accepted amongst Christians involved in cross-cultural ministry. The principles of contextualisation can be used in pastoral situations. It requires that we are very careful to understand the important issues and questions raised by any pastoral situation, which may be unique, and then to use the Bible in a way that responds to those realities.

The skill required by the pastoral practitioner is to be able to understand the pastoral situation well enough so that we can identify how biblical insights illuminate that specific situation in a way that takes into account the needs, backgrounds, concerns, aspirations etc. of those we are working with. It is about making judgements of appropriateness rather than applying ready-made solutions that have worked for us.

Activity 5b (I/G): Practising contextualisation in a pastoral situation

We are used to thinking in terms of the question and the answer. Try, however, thinking in terms of situation and question. Write a number of modern situations on one side of cards/pieces of paper. On the back of each card write some of the questions that the situation poses or issues that have to be considered if this situation is to be properly understood. Having identified the questions and issues, jot down some relevant biblical material that offers appropriate insights.

Activity 5b (G)

The individual activity can be used with a group. Or write a series of modern situations on cards and place them face down on the table or floor. In turn, members of the groups turn them over and read them out. The group then has to think of questions the situation might generate (e.g. cohabitation raises the question of whether you have to go through a wedding ceremony to be married in the eyes of God). To add a bit of fun, run this 'quiz style', awarding points for each question raised and only allowing a short time for each situation. Then identify relevant biblical material for each situation that helps with the questions and issues raised.

Feedback

This is one of my cards.

Situation
The development of nuclear weapons

Question
Is it right to develop weapons of mass destruction that would have long-term consequences for generations to come and for the environment?

Some of the biblical material

Not wiping out a whole population (Amos 1:11)
The earth as God's (Psalm 24:1–2)
Stewardship (Genesis 1:26–28)

Reflection

John Stott writes about 'double listening', describing it as 'the faculty of listening to two voices at the same time, the voice of God through Scripture and the voices of the men and women around us'. Stott identifies Job's comforters as people who failed to be double listeners. He says of them 'they did not really listen to what Job had to say. They merely repeated their own thoughtless and heartless claptrap'. Can you identify times when you have been an effective double listener and times when you have repeated your own claptrap? Record your thoughts in your reflective diary.

Final reflection

Go back to the key question and think through your response. Think of two ways in which your use of the Bible might change as a result of your studying this unit. Record your thoughts in your reflective diary.

Review

When you have finished this unit you should be able to:

◆ explain some of the processes involved in interpreting and applying the Bible
◆ describe the roles of the three 'conversation partners' in biblical application
◆ use the Bible to question your 'taken for granted' assumptions
◆ comment on the strengths and weaknesses of the model of application used in the unit.

Assess the degree to which you think you have achieved each of these.

Resources

Anderson, H. and Foley, E. (1998) *Mighty Stories – Dangerous Rituals: Weaving Together the Human and Divine*. Jossey-Bass.

Ballard, P. and Holmes, S. R. (eds) (2005) *The Bible in Pastoral Practice*. Darton, Longman and Todd. Part II looks at the way scholarship affects the interpretation of the Bible.

Borg, M. (2001) *Reading the Bible Again for the First Time*. HarperCollins.

Briggs, R. (2003) *Reading the Bible Wisely*. Baker Academic.

Fowl, S. (1998) *Engaging Scripture – A Model for Theological Interpretation*. Blackwells.

Oliver, G. (2006) *Holy Bible, Human Bible: Questions Pastoral Practice Must Ask*. Darton, Longman and Todd. Section 7–8.

Pattison. S. 'Some Straw for the Bricks: A Basic Introduction to Theological Reflection' in *The Blackwell Reader in Pastoral and Practical Theology*. Woodward, J. and Pattison. S. (eds) (2000) Blackwell Publishing Ltd.

Rooms, N. (2005) 'Inculturation Comes Home: Lessons from the Worldwide Church' in *Anvil* Vol. 22:4.

www.bibinterp.com
www.bibicalstudies.org.uk Select 'Bible' then 'Interpretation'
www.findarticles.com Search by 'Biblical interpretation' using free articles
www.religion-online.org Select 'The authority of the Bible'
www.virtualrel.net Select 'Biblical studies'
www.bible-researcher.com Select 'Biblical Interpretation and Theology'.

Unit 6

When the Bible makes faith difficult

Key question

How can I deal with Bible passages that make faith difficult for some people?

1. Introduction

John Hick was a committed 'Christian Union' Christian whilst at University. However, his experience as a young man led him to conclude that 'my earlier views seemed a little naïve in some ways'. He found it impossible to continue to believe what he perceived to be the traditional biblical position on salvation, concluding that it meant that people's eternal destiny depended on an accident of birth. Hick is an example of a liberal Christian who found that one interpretation of certain Bible texts made Christian faith difficult.

Likewise, John Wenham, who was a well-known evangelical leader committed to the authority of the Bible, once wrote: '"Look at the goodness of God" says the Christian teacher. But when we look into the Bible things seem far from good. The book contains many horrors.' Unlike Hick, Wenham held to his evangelical commitment all his life. But he still grappled with certain passages of the Bible which he found very troubling.

Reflection

Think of people you know who have either left church or changed what they believed because some biblical stories or texts made faith difficult for them. How could they have been helped to keep their faith? Record your thoughts in your reflective diary.

2. Texts of Terror

In the research project some practitioners stressed the negative impact that some texts can have. *Texts of Terror* is the title of an influential book by Phyllis Trible in which she discusses four Bible passages describing truly shocking incidents. Here we are drawing on the notion of 'texts of terror' in the wider sense of biblical passages that raise hard questions which make faith difficult for some readers. We will call them 'troubling texts'.

Activity 2 (I/G): Identifying troubling texts

> *The women's discussion group got heated and Alena became very upset about St Paul's teaching on marriage. Why should wives submit to husbands? Apart from being discriminatory and old-fashioned, didn't it encourage a passive attitude? In a fit of frustration Alena crossed out the offending verses. A few weeks later a friend, Heather, came round for coffee. She picked up Alena's Bible lying on top of the fridge, opened it, saw the crossing out and smiled. 'I thought you Christians were not allowed to do that,' she joked.*

Many people, like Alena, have texts they would like to cross out of the Bible because they create barriers to faith.

a. Imagine that you are putting together a selection of Bible passages for a new Christian. Note down some of the texts/stories that you would definitely leave off your list on the grounds that they might make faith difficult or even be 'texts of terror' for some.

b. Now select one of these texts. Imagine that you have the opportunity to write a memo to God headed: 'Why did you include this passage in the Bible?' Write up to 100 words honestly explaining the difficulties that this text causes you.

Activity 2 (G)

Follow the individual activity, but each member can contribute one troubling text. The group can then either work together on writing the memo for one text or be sub-divided with each sub-group working on one text. The resulting memos can be discussed by the whole group.

Note: The use of difficult texts with children is explored in unit 12.

Feedback

a. Some suggestions of texts that I would not include in a selection for young Christians are:

Job 1: God seems to be 'playing' with people.
Judges 3:12–30: The death of Ehud.
Judges 19: The Levite's concubine.
Joshua 6: The slaughter after the fall of Jericho.
Genesis 19:1–11: Lot and the visitor.
Psalm 137:8–9: Unacceptable vengeance.
Matthew 15:21–28: Jesus appearing to call a Gentile woman 'a dog'.
Matthew 17:24–27: The coin in the fish's mouth. This sounds like a fairy tale.

b. Memo to God

> Why were the stories of the Levite's concubine and Lot and the visitor allowed to stay in the Bible when the Church decided the canon? They are not only offensive and upsetting but provide non-believers with ammunition.

3. Interpreting troubling texts

Troubling texts raise an important theological question in the pastoral situation: should the pastor allow someone to interpret a text they find challenging in any way they are comfortable with, or should the pastor guide their interpretation of the text? To put it another way, can we say that any interpretation goes in using the Bible in Christian ministry? Look at the case study on Genesis 3, a text that troubles many Christians because of the curse on humankind that follows one couple's fall.

A wide variety of people had come to the Alpha group and the subject of 'the fall' (Genesis 3) came up. The leader wanted to highlight human rebellion against God. A humanist in the group found the story extremely illuminating; he suggested that it reflected the moment of liberation for the human race, the point at which humans discovered that they could decide for themselves.

Activity 3 (I): Defining the limits for interpreting troubling texts

An important question raised by this incident is this: 'At what point does an interpretation which helps someone make sense of a troubling text become an inappropriate use of the Bible?' How we answer this affects pastoral practice.

Find a chair where you can make yourself comfortable and imagine yourself leading this Alpha group. What would your response be to the humanist? Imagine how the conversation would proceed. What emotions would the humanist have experienced? Would you have 'honoured' their interpretation of this text in the way that you handled it?

Option: Using the tools

Having spent a few minutes in this 'imagination mode', ask yourself whether you have used any of the following tools, dealt with elsewhere in this workbook (see below) to help in thinking through a response to this case study? If so, which have you found particularly helpful?

a. The idea of pastoral practice as a conversation between the Bible, the individual and the situation (unit 5 section 3).
b. The idea that indwelling the story is an appropriate way of achieving an authentic but faithful application of the Bible (unit 2 section 4).
c. The three ways in which the Bible might function as an authority (unit 4 section 3).

Activity 3 (G)

As for the individual activity, but two people can role-play the Alpha group and then be 'hot seated' (asked probing questions while still in role) by the rest of the group. Alternatively, role-playing in pairs, group members construct a 'silent conversation' between the humanist and the person leading the Alpha group. To do this you divide a piece of paper in two – as in the feedback. The leader writes the first response in their column. The paper is then passed between the pair several times. Each person writes a response to the other person's comment as the paper is passed back and forth and the conversation develops. Passing the paper and writing gives time for thought and response. The group together can then discuss how their conversations developed and the different responses to the humanist's contribution.

Feedback

This is how my conversation developed.

Bible study leader	Humanist
That's the second time I have heard the passage interpreted like that.	Who else thinks like that?
I heard a writer say the same thing once.	How did you respond?
I was a bit taken aback. I had never looked at the story like that.	Have you changed how you think about the story?
No, I haven't. I still think it is a story about a broken relationship and the beginning of things going wrong.	Couldn't it be more about 'coming of age'?
If we have 'come of age' we have made a bit of a mess by making all the decisions ourselves.	But at least it is *our* mess.

4. Possible theological responses to troubling texts

The fate of those who have died is an example of a troubling theological question arising from the Bible. Look at two of the biblical texts, Matthew 13:36–43 and Matthew 25:31–46. Traditional Christian teaching on hell has made some people question the nature of God when it seems that he consigns people to eternal suffering for not believing 'properly'. C. S. Lewis said of it, 'There is no doctrine which I would more willingly remove from Christianity than this, but it has the full support of Scripture and, specially, of our Lord's own words.'

There are a number of possible theological responses to troubling texts, such as the doctrine of hell, which can be offered to people in pastoral situations. The are summarised below. You may be able to think of others, if so add them to the list.

a. Accept the texts literally or as traditionally interpreted in order to maintain belief in the traditional biblical teaching and swallow any objections. Ultimately this will mean accepting that wrath and justice are part of God's nature and his response to unrepentant humans. Any discomfort with the doctrine is submitted to the higher authority of the biblical text.

b. Take into account the style and genre (unit 2) of the texts. How much is symbolism? How much is rhetoric or hyperbole? Are these troubling passages designed to challenge rather than being doctrinal statements? How far can you press the details of a parable such as Matthew 25:31–46 or apocalyptic literature such as Revelation?

c. Where appropriate, reinterpret the texts in some way so that the view of God entailed by them becomes more in line with what is perceived to be the message of the rest of Scripture. The literal or traditional meaning is not then seen to be their proper meaning. Maybe the way these texts have been traditionally interpreted owes more medieval imagery than to biblical doctrine? For example, some evangelicals, most famously John Wenham and John Stott, argue that the Bible doesn't actually teach eternal, conscious punishment, but rather what is called 'conditionalism'. By this is meant that only the saved enjoy a conscious existence after death. The lost simply cease to exist. Eternal life is therefore *conditional* on a right response to God.

d. Reinterpret the troubling texts as human reflections on the nature of God rather than revelation from God; these passages then cease to be a problem. Eternal conscious suffering of the lost is regarded as the way people in the past understood God's judgement, but this is no longer seen as acceptable and is rejected in the light of modern understandings of God's justice and compassion. This is not to reject the Bible as a sacred text, but it is to regard the Bible as having human, not divine, origins.

Activity 4 (I): Assessing the pastoral consequences

Each of the positions a.-d. has pastoral consequences when used in ministry. Using a table (see the feedback), list at least one negative pastoral consequence and one positive pastoral consequence for each of the strategies for dealing with troubling texts. Which strategies do you use? Do you always use this strategy or does it depend on the context? What might cause you to change strategy?

Option: Making connections

Look at the four positions/strategies and work out how they relate to the three views of the Bible described in unit 4.

Activity 4 (G)

Use the individual activity with group members working on their own responses and then sharing them. Alternatively construct a large version of the table on flip chart paper and complete it as a group discussion.

Feedback

We differed in the group, but the majority tended to use b. or c. This is our chart.

Options	Negative pastoral consequences	Positive pastoral consequences
a. Accept the texts at face value.	Buries doubts. Ignores the fact that lots of people have problems with certain texts. It becomes difficult to integrate faith and doubts.	Simple, clear and secure. May help some Christians to be accepted by their community. This could make people think about eternity. Could lead to conversion.
b. Interpret according to style and genre.	There is sometimes a difficulty in deciding the style and genre.	Gives a feeling of treating the Bible with integrity.
c. Reinterpret the texts in the light of the whole Bible.	Could shake people's general acceptance of the Bible. May be too difficult for those without training.	Could lead to people wanting to widen biblical knowledge. Enables you to hold the difficult parts in balance with others.
d. Reinterpret the texts as human speculation.	Leaves believers without reference points or boundaries. May not encourage faith.	A sense of release from believing immoral things. An antidote to 'one text' theology.

Reflection

As a pastoral practitioner you will have to decide whether:

a. you will take a particular line when dealing with troubling texts and not inform people of other possibilities.

b. you offer your own view but also make people aware of the different possibilities for handling these texts.

5. The pastoral challenge

The pastoral challenge presented by troubling texts is that they can create what John Hull has described as 'cognitive dissonance', an internal conflict of beliefs. Put simply this means a feeling that one is required to believe in something, for example the eternal conscious punishment of the unbeliever in hell, that conflicts with one's other beliefs, for example that God is loving and compassionate. Hull suggests that this experience can cause considerable stress and he maps various responses to this. They are summarised below (you may like to add more of your own):

a. *The Child-like Response.* In this case the person cannot cope with the struggle of dealing with the conflict, so decides to trust others, particularly church leaders, to tell him/her what to believe. Energy is invested in keeping busy with church activity rather than thinking through the conflict. Often the troubling texts are ignored by churches, never mentioned in sermons, never used in worship and never covered in Bible studies. Hull sees the danger of this response in being the surfacing of the conflict later in life, particularly at crisis points, with the possible collapse of faith.

b. *The Hardened Response.* In this case the person becomes an uncompromising believer and ceases to feel the conflict. Hull sees the danger of this response in being the development of tribal attitudes where other viewpoints are seen as a threat. The prognosis for social harmony and citizenship in plural societies is not good if this attitude prevails.

c. *The Bargaining Response.* This third option is Hull's preferred one. It entails the person being able to negotiate between their own experience and the texts that they find troublesome such that an inner harmony is achieved and the tension is resolved. In some cases this will mean rejecting the troubling texts, as for example some feminists do in the case of Pauline teaching on the relationship between husbands and wives in Ephesians 5.

Hull suggested three responses, but I think there is a fourth possibility. Another way of responding is to choose to live with the troubling nature of the text. The text is accepted as an anomaly, one that we don't comprehend as it seems to contradict other biblical texts. It is not dismissed as there is always the possibility that a) we are misunderstanding the text or b) it will make sense at some future time. It is treated like the results of a science experiment that contradicts accepted ideas. The contradictory data is not abandoned; it is kept because the theory may be refined and then the data will make sense. This attitude of mind requires the ability to live with unresolved questions and conflict of beliefs.

Activity 5 (I): Mental images for conflict of beliefs

Many Christians find conflict of beliefs difficult to accept. One suggestion is that this is because they have an unhelpful mental picture of conflict; they see it as akin to a tug of war where there are always winners and losers. Try suggesting another mental image that will make it easier for people to see conflict of beliefs as something positive, one of life's ambiguities that can be accepted. You might like to do this visually, creating images to express your ideas.

Activity 5 (G)

Use the individual activity but provide pens, pencils and large sheets of paper so that group members can then work on images together.

Feedback

Two positive ways of looking at conflict that I have found helpful are:

a. Conflict of belief is like the grit in an oyster. It is a constant irritation, but it can produce the pearl.

b. Conflict of belief is like the tension in the guy ropes of a tent. It is always there, but without it the tent would not stand up.

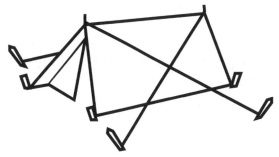

Final reflection

Spend a few moments thinking about the issues this unit has raised for you. In what ways has it offered you new possibilities in this difficult area? How would you now respond to the key question at the beginning of the unit? Record your thoughts in your reflective diary.

Review

When you have finished this unit you should be able to:

♦ describe your own reaction to troubling biblical texts that pose challenges to faith.
♦ explain a range of theological responses to such texts.
♦ offer practical strategies to others who are challenged by these texts.

Assess the degree to which you think you have achieved each of these.

Resources

Bennett-Moore, Z. (2002) *Introducing Feminist Perspectives on Pastoral Theology.* Sheffield Academic Press.

Borg, M. (2001) *Reading the Bible Again for the First Time.* HarperCollins.

Evangelical Alliance (2000) *The Nature of Hell.* ACUTE.

Gomes, P. J. (1996) *The Good Book: Reading the Bible with Mind and Heart.* HarperCollins.

Hick, J. (2003) *An Autobiography.* One World Publications.

Hull, J. (1985) *What Prevents Christian Adults from Learning?* SCM Press.

Lewis, C. S. (1977) *The Problem of Pain.* Fount.

Rowland, C. and Corner, M. (1990) *Liberating Exegesis – The Challenge of Liberation Theology to Biblical Studies.* SPCK.

Trible, P. (1984), *Texts of Terror.* Fortress Press.

Wenham, J. (1974) *The Goodness of God.* Inter-Varsity Press.

www.religion-online.org Select 'The authority of the Bible'
www.findarticles.com Search by 'Difficult Bible texts' using free articles
www.ntgateway.com Books and articles on specific texts
www.otgateway.com Books and articles on specific texts
www.bibicalstudies.org.uk Select 'Bible' then 'Interpretation'

Unit 7

Metaphors, the Bible and Christian ministry

Key question

How does my use of metaphors *for* the Bible and *from* the Bible affect my use of the text in my pastoral practice?

Preparation

You will need access to the internet for the art activity, or a book could be used instead but this might involve a trip to the library (page 75).

Note: the words 'metaphor' and 'image' are used here to cover *all* non-literal language.

1. Introduction

We all use images in everyday language when, for example, we talk of people going 'as white as a sheet'. Such images affect not only how we think but also what we do. If doctors think of bodies only as machines, medicine can become very impersonal and doctors start to think like engineers. This unit will help you assess the way you use biblical images and how metaphors in general affect your approach to ministry.

Metaphors used to be thought of as little more than verbal decoration but they are much more than that. They are ways of communicating that carry a huge amount of meaning in a few words. To use a boxing term, they punch above their weight. Metaphors make demands of us, challenging us to see life in a particular way. For example, the image of life as a pathway (Psalm 119:35; Matthew 7:13–14) challenges us not only to find the pathway but to stay on it.

When we talk about the Bible we often use images such as a sword, a guide, and a finger pointing to God. But it is not always easy to spot these metaphors for sometimes they are used implicitly. If someone says, 'We need to stand firm on the Bible,' they are implying that the Bible is like a foundation. We need to listen for the images we use both explicitly and implicitly, for images affect our practice. For example, if we view the Bible primarily as a hammer (Jeremiah 23:29), do we begin to see every problem as a nail and react accordingly?

Activity 1 (I): Which biblical images of the Word do I use?

Here is a list of images which relate to the Word of God:

◆ Rain: Isaiah 55:10–11
◆ Sword: Ephesians 6:17; Hebrews 4:12
◆ Hammer: Jeremiah 23:29

- ◆ Fire: Jeremiah 23:29
- ◆ Seed: Mark 4:1–9, 13–20
- ◆ Food: Hebrews 5:12–14; Psalm 119:103
- ◆ Light: Psalm 119:105

Tick or highlight the images on the list above with appropriate coloured pen/pencils (see below). Give a one-sentence reason for each of your choices:

    a. Yellow: favourite
    b. Red: least favourite
    c. Black: most useful pastorally
    d. Blue: least useful pastorally

Activity 1 (G)

Follow the individual activity, but place the words from the list of images on separate cards on the floor or table. Give each group member coloured counters (yellow, red, black, blue) to place on the cards rather than tick them. Look at the results and explore any patterns that emerge. Is there an image that everyone avoids? Why? Are there favourite images that everyone has put a counter on? Why? Ask people to give reasons for their choices. Use this as the basis for discussion.

Feedback

    a. Our group liked rain and food most with their associations with growth and refreshment.
    b. Fire and hammer were our least favourite images as we felt they were too negative.
    c. Light was thought to be most useful pastorally as it gives a sense of guidance but has layered meanings to explore.
    d. The hammer was felt to be least useful pastorally as it has connotations of violence and force.

2. The right word in the right place

> *The preacher held up a Bible, its black covers flopped open and its gold edges fanned. 'This is the Word of God,' he stated confidently as he held the Bible aloft, 'God's manual for everyday living'. The congregation reacted in different ways to this metaphor.*
>
> *Andrew wondered what the Bible had to say to his situation. He was deeply concerned about animal rights and the use of animals in medical research.*
>
> *A few rows back Tom nodded and smiled; he had often gone to the Bible and found in its pages the help he needed when coping with the problems and joys of three teenage children.*
>
> *Laura looked puzzled. As a doctor she was confronted by situations unknown to the Bible: how could she find help when thinking about stem cell research?*
>
> *Next to her sat Megan who was visiting the church for the first time. She had picked up a Gideon Bible in a hotel. Inside the front cover she had found a list of subjects with references. She had looked up some of them and found comfort in the words she read. She had come to church to find out more.*

Metaphors, such as the 'manual' in the case study, set up certain expectations and can affect how we handle the text. If we see the Bible as a manual, we may expect that we can simply look up answers to life's problems. This might lead to the Bible being handled as an answer book without engaging with its wider message. Although the Bible does contain answers, and there are times we can look up passages that speak directly to our situation, we cannot treat the whole book as if it is a trouble-shooting manual.

Activity 2 (I): Choosing a suitable metaphor

a. Look at the case study. In what ways is the authority of the Bible communicated? Look at the following things in the case study:

 ◆ the type of Bible used.
 ◆ the preacher's gestures.
 ◆ the manual metaphor itself.

b. What is positive about this metaphor? What might be negative?

c. Look at the list of biblical metaphors on page 70 and select one. Draw a radial diagram (see feedback). Write your chosen metaphor in the centre circle. In the outer circles, describe:

 ◆ the expectations this metaphor might create.
 ◆ how it might affect the way the Bible is used.
 ◆ a pastoral situation where this might be a good choice of metaphor (give reasons why it would be suitable in that situation).
 ◆ a pastoral situation where this might be an unsuitable metaphor (give reasons why it would be unsuitable in that situation).

Activity 2 (G)

Follow the individual activity, but use a.–b. as discussion questions. Draw the diagram on a large sheet of paper and fill it in together. You may wish to try more than one metaphor.

Feedback

a. The black and gold nature of the Bible itself gives it a look of authority. The fact that it is held high reinforces its status. The manual image conveys authority as we expect a manual to be written by an expert from the manufacturer.

b. Positive: reliability and relevance. This could be positive for believers and chime with their experience.
Negative: although you can go to the Bible for 'answers' there are some situations that are complex or new that cannot be solved using this approach. This could lead to people feeling unnecessarily let down. It could also discourage emotionally engaged reading.

c. I chose the metaphor 'food' for my diagram.

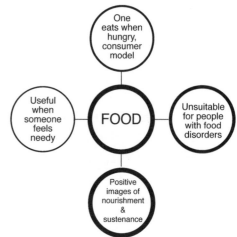

3. New metaphors

Christians are not restricted to using metaphors for the Bible that are found in the text itself. (The image of a 'manual for life' is not found in the text.) However, any new metaphors do need to be in line with the overall message of the Bible. In the research project it was found that people used images such as a 'tool', 'spring', 'foundation' and 'treasure chest', each implying a different use.

Reflection

There are some metaphors that are central to the Christian faith that reflect the world of the first century. For example, 'atonement' reflects the sacrificial system and 'redemption' reflects a society where slavery was prevalent. Can these metaphors ever be updated or have they special status?

Activity 3 (I): Can new images affect the way we use the Bible?

Choose two or more images from the list that follows and, without thinking too much, jot down your immediate reactions to them. When you have done this, think about how this image might alter the way you use the Bible in Christian ministry.

Images of the Bible

In his book *Holy Bible, Human Bible*, Gordon Oliver suggests a variety of metaphors for the Bible:

◆ the Bible as a stranger whom you invite into your life.
◆ the Bible as the host who invites you in.
◆ the Bible as a wild animal that is let loose in the world.
◆ the Bible as a gift from God.
◆ the Bible as a soap opera.

Activity 3 (G)

Follow the individual activity, but write the images on cards or enlarge the pictures provided and add their titles. Place them face down on the floor, then turn them over one at a time and ask the group to call out their immediate response.

Gift   Stranger   Host   Soap opera   Wild animal

Feedback

The Bible as stranger: interesting, exciting, the anticipation of new experiences. This could encourage me to have a sense of expectancy when using the Bible with people.

The Bible as wild animal: unpredictable and slightly dangerous but exciting. It may help reduce the tendency to domesticate the Bible and take it for granted when it really needs to disturb. It may make me more open to using difficult texts with people (unit 6).

The Bible as gift from God: friendly and joyful and encouraging rather than convicting. I would use this when wanting to emphasise God's love and grace.

4. Metaphors as bridges

Metaphors connect thinking and feeling, creating a bridge between the two by triggering associations in our thoughts and emotions. If we think about God as a potter, this starts a train of thoughts in our minds about God as creator and shaper and ourselves as clay. This in turn stimulates emotions and thoughts concerning control and freedom. A good metaphor gives rise to an open-ended series of associations. For example, when we think about God as potter and ourselves as clay we consider the role of a potter and the properties of clay and our personal experience of those things. We may have experienced making pots, know the feeling of clay, have read about potters, seen them on television or watched demonstrations. Metaphors forge a connection between our lives and the Bible's message.

The way that the metaphors link feeling, thinking and experience and create open-ended associations is both a strength and weakness. Images may encourage variety and depth of thought and feeling but if someone latches onto an image as part of a dysfunctional emotional response, it can stunt growth rather than facilitate it. Sometimes people need to move on in the images they relate to.

A good metaphor can't be reduced to prose, as too much of the bridge-building power to make connections is lost. It is not like losing an illustration that is not integral to the text. In the pastoral context, an appropriate biblical image can have more impact than prose because it touches both head and heart. In our Christian ministry we need to make sure we are aware of the range of images the Bible uses and integrate these into our pastoral practice rather than sticking to a few well-worn ones. We can also create our own images as we seek to help others to explore the significance of the Bible's message.

Activity 4 (I): What do we lose when we remove metaphors?

Take an extract from one of your favourite psalms that has lots of images and reduce it to prose. What is lost in terms of thinking and feeling?

Activity 4 (G)

As for the individual activity, but decide on a section of a psalm to do together. Read the poetry version followed by the prose.

Feedback

Psalm 46:1–3: God is near, protecting and strengthening when we are in trouble so there is no need to be frightened even though the worst happens.

Reducing this to prose has lost all the emotions associated with running for refuge. It also misses the terror which is built up by the poetic images. As a result it sounds more like escapism than faith shouted defiantly into the storm. In terms of thinking, the images convey the fact that we are not spared the storm but God is present in it.

5. Two worlds

Metaphors put two very different worlds side by side: the world of the biblical image and our world. We cannot, however, just uproot metaphors from the text, plant them in a modern pastoral situation and assume they apply in the same way. We may use the same words but the change of time and culture can change meanings. For example, Psalm 139:1–12 uses a range of images to describe God's knowledge and omni-presence. There is an element that could be seen as negative ('Where can I go from your Spirit?'...) but this is balanced by verse 10 that speaks of God's guidance and care. Talking in the same terms today *without explanation* may invoke associations of Orwell's 'Big Brother' and the surveillance society which are largely negative and sometimes downright sinister. We need to think about the original culture, what the text meant in that context and what the author may have intended to convey (unit 5).

The original web of ideas and meanings attached to a biblical image should be reflected in our own use of the text in order to make sure that we are using the image with integrity (see unit 5). We always have to bear in mind the two worlds: the world of the Bible and our world, if we are to remain both relevant and yet faithful to the text.

Activity 5 (I): Importing the biblical images into our world

There is an artistic tradition that puts together a story or image from the Bible and a 'modern' scene. Often the image from the Bible is shown as a picture hanging on a wall or a as a view through a window. The viewer is meant to meditate on the relation-ship between these two. For an example go to www.nationalgallery.org.uk, search for Velázquez and look for 'Christ in the House of Martha and Mary' (this example uses a story rather than an image but the technique is the same). Alternatively, look up this painting in your local library.

Create your own picture for meditation that brings together the two worlds – an image from the Bible e.g. 'The Light of the World' and the modern world. See the feedback for an example. In the small rectangle, which represents the picture on the wall, write or draw your biblical image. In the larger area draw or write notes on a modern situation to which this biblical image has something to say. Before you draw or write, check that you understand how the image is being used in the Bible and think about how the image might be understood today.

Activity 5 (G)

Create a picture as a group discussing what goes into each section.

Feedback

I used the image of the 'bruised reed' from Isaiah.

> # Someone lovingly restoring a derelict house
>
> ## 'a bruised reed he will not break'
>
> God is on the side of the person who struggles with life, even if it is their fault.

6. Handle with care

> *Samina went to church with a feeling of sadness and dread for the future. The second Gulf War had just broken out and she was strongly opposed to it. For the first time she noticed the military metaphors in the hymns which seemed to be full of terms such as 'battle', 'war' and 'soldier'. Samina stayed silent. She felt she could not join in.*

Care is needed when using biblical images in pastoral situations: what is helpful for one person may create a barrier for another. What is a useful image for understanding God or salvation may not help in other situations. For example, describing the Christian life as a race is not helpful for someone suffering from stress at work in a highly competitive environment. Distortion can also occur if one image is over-emphasised or used to the exclusion of others. For example, if we over emphasise the Holy Spirit as comforter, we might ignore his ethical demands. Images challenge as well as console.

The feelings and ideas people associate with metaphors vary, according to their gender, age, culture and life experience. The same metaphor can communicate different things to different people. We need to be sensitive and aware of how people might be experiencing the metaphors we use. For example, God as Father is a negative metaphor for some. This does not mean it cannot be used, but God's fatherhood needs expounding so that people are aware of ways in which God is like and yet unlike a human father.

Metaphors are like torches that shine a light on some aspects of a subject but not others. For example, 'God is like a rock' is true only in so far as God is strong and dependable, it does not mean God is as hard as stone. This partial quality of metaphors means we probably need to use a variety to ensure appropriate balance.

Activity 6 (I): Associations and misunderstandings

Choose one metaphor for God that you use in your Christian ministry, then write the associations you have with that image inside the outline of a head (see feedback). What room for misunderstanding is there for you? You may want to repeat this exercise with a friend to see what their associations are.

Activity 6 (G)

Take a sheet of A4 paper and, on the first line, write one metaphor for God that is often used in Christian ministry, for example God as king. The piece of paper is passed to the first person in the group who reads aloud the metaphor, then silently writes their own associations with that metaphor (it needs to be ones they are happy to share). The top of the paper is then folded over by the first person so that it cannot be seen. The paper is passed to the next person who adds their associations with the same metaphor and folds over the paper. Repeat this until all the group have had a chance to write something, then unroll the paper and read the results. Use the results as the basis of discussion picking up the issues in this section.

Feedback

The king metaphor could be misunderstood if it were thought of in terms of modern kings with symbolic roles and little power. A king could also be misunderstood as a distant figure who is only interested in the grand scheme of things and not in day-to-day matters.

Final reflection

Go back to the key question and think about your answer. Reflect on what you have studied in this unit:

◆ what surprised or puzzled you?
◆ what excited you?
◆ what aspect would you like to explore further?

Record your thoughts in your reflective diary.

Review

As a result of studying this unit you should now be able to:

◆ explain how the images used to describe the role of the Bible may affect pastoral practice.
◆ articulate new metaphors for the Bible and describe your response to them.
◆ describe your own use of metaphors and some of the issues surrounding the use of metaphors in Christian ministry.

Resources

Astley, J. (2004) *Exploring God-Talk: Using Language in Religion*. Darton, Longman and Todd.
Borg, M. (2001) *Reading the Bible Again for the First Time*. HarperCollins.
Lakoff, J. and Johnson, M. (1980) *Metaphors We Live By*. University of Chicago Press.

Ortony, A. (1993) *Metaphor and Thought* (second edition). Cambridge University Press.

Oliver, G. (2006). *Holy Bible, Human Bible: Questions Pastoral Practice Must Ask*. Darton, Longman and Todd.

Nouwen, H. (1972/2005) *Wounded Healer.* Darton, Longman and Todd.

Ryken, L. (1998) *Dictionary of Biblical Imagery*. Inter-Varsity Press.

Ryken, L. (1996) *Words of Delight: a Literary Introduction to the Bible* (second edition). Baker Book House.

Smith, D. and Shortt, J. (2002) *The Bible and the Task of Teaching*. The Stapleford Centre. See the chapter on metaphor.

Tidball, D. (1999) *Builders and Fools – Leadership the Bible Way*. Inter-Varsity Press.

www.intervarsity.org Search by 'Metaphor'

www.bible-researcher.com Search by 'Biblical imagery'

www.biblicalstudies.org.uk Select 'Bible', then 'Interpretation', then 'Idioms'

www.ekklesia.co.uk search by 'Biblical imagery'

www.findarticles.com search by 'Biblical metaphor'

Unit 8

The Bible, the pastor and the person

Key question

How can a deeper understanding of people and how they differ help me to use the Bible appropriately in Christian ministry?

Preparation

You may wish to do the activity on page 84 before the session if you are working with a group.

1. Introduction

The people we encounter in pastoral contexts are not blank slates; in any pastoral situation where the Bible is used there is a 'conversation' between the pastor, the person, the situation and the Bible (page 56). The research project reflected participants' concern to make pastoral encounters a conversation or dialogue. They spoke of sensitive listening and not imposing the Bible on people by use of power and position.

This unit focuses on the experience of receiving pastoral care in order that those involved in pastoral situations can develop appropriate ways of using the Bible. We are all both subjects and objects in relationships. In this unit, we will particularly explore the objective end of the spectrum of relationship, where the experience of receiving or using the services and care of others is paramount. We will explore five aspects of being human that are significant in pastoral situations.

Reflection

Think of an occasion when you experienced someone else's pastoral ministry. What was it like? How did you feel being the recipient? Were you taken seriously as a person? Were you made to feel you had something to give? Could you use the Bible in this situation or was it only used by the 'pastor'? Record your thoughts in your reflective diary.

2. Faith history

The Bible is full of stories of people who are on a journey of faith, but each story is different: St Paul's faith journey was different from Timothy's and Jacob's. Not only are we all at different stages, we all travel a different route and begin from different starting points. The end product, too, will be suitably varied. The experiences that have

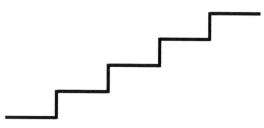

shaped our faith journey and where we are on that journey will affect how we respond to the Bible and how we use the Bible with others. If we imagine faith as a linear journey where everyone starts at the same place but reaches different stages, it might look like a staircase with people on various steps.

If we allow for many different routes *as well* as stages we would have to construct a different diagram. Are all the routes equivalent? Is the middle stage on one route the same as a middle stage on another?

Activity 2 (I): The journey of faith

◆ Create a diagram that you think reflects your journey of faith and mark on it key events that affected your attitude to the Bible.
◆ Create a diagram that reflects the varied nature of peoples' faith journeys and their different starting and finishing points.

Activity 2 (G)

As for the individual activity but compare diagrams, if people are happy to do that.

Feedback

My faith-journey diagram

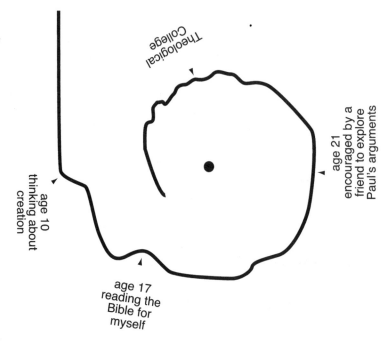

Reflection

Think about your ministry and reflect on the following:

◆ where in my ministry do I need to be sensitive to people's different faith journeys?
◆ do I imply an acceptance of varied faith journeys or a single route by what I say and do?
◆ how could I use the Bible to affirm people's varied routes of faith?

Record your thoughts in your reflective diary.

3. Differing Ideals

What people imagine as the 'ideal' mature Christian differs, but whatever our ideal it will affect how we respond to people in pastoral practice and how we use the Bible. If our ideal of a mature, strong Christian is someone who has a deep relationship with God then the relational side of the Bible may be stressed. If our ideal Christian is someone with a wide biblical knowledge, then clearly biblical knowledge may be stressed. This sounds obvious, but sometimes we are unaware of our ideal and its influence on our use of the Bible.

Activity 3 (I/G): Describing the ideal

Inside the outline of a person list up to six words or phrases that make up your ideal of the mature Christian?

Feedback

Compassionate, practising the presence of God, balanced, interacts with the Bible.

Reflection

Sometimes people have an explicit ideal (something they say they aim for) but their practice tells a different story. If someone looked at your practice, particularly your use of the Bible, could they tell what your ideal Christian was like?

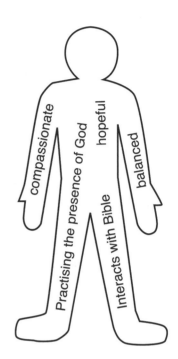

4. Faith Development

Thomas Groome, an American researcher into faith development, defined faith as attitudes (relationship), content (beliefs) and actions (lifestyle). For Groome faith is: 'believing, trusting and doing'. In pastoral encounters we need to give full weight to all these aspects of faith or people may feel that only one aspect is valued.

James Fowler is a leading figure amongst those who research faith development. He defined faith in terms of *how* it was held, not *what* was believed, for the same belief may be held in different ways during a person's life. Fowler sees faith development as a series of stages that follow each other in an upward, linear movement (others disagree with him over this). This development is not something that happens automatically, like physical growth; it can be triggered by new experiences and challenges. The Bible can be part of that challenge, offering people new ways of thinking and presenting them with challenging ways of living and being. Fowler sees people progressing through six stages. The first three stages are described on pages 101–2 and the last three stages are detailed below. (An adult congregation may include stages 2 and 3.) One of the insights that came from Fowler is that the movement between stages often involves a period of uncertainty and questioning. This can be exciting for some and unnerving for others, and how leaders react is crucial. Such questioning can be the sign of a growing faith, not a declining one. Leaders need to explore how they handle such situations in order to encourage growth. The following stage descriptions are basic, more details can be found at:

www.jmm.aaa.net.au/articles/2219.htm
www.faculty.plts.edu/gpence/html/flowler.htm
www.en.wikipedia.org/wiki/Stages_of_faith_development
www.reality.org.nz/articles/33/33-pritchard.asp

Note: Criticisms of Fowler's view of faith development can be found in the resources.

Stage 4

This stage is about people developing their own identity and ideology. The person develops as an individual and no longer depends on others to define who they are and how they view the world. At stage 4 people are less afraid of being distinctive. Symbols of faith are translated into ideas and concepts as these can be handled abstractly. This stage is often precipitated by leaving home, starting a new job, the death of a parent, divorce or some other significant event concerning important relationships.

Stage 5

At stage 5 people are comfortable with their place in the world and feel able to explore without feeling insecure. At this stage people take the initiative in seeking truth even if what they find is challenging as they recognise the complexity of life. At stage 5 people recognise the partial nature of things and are able to open themselves to varied traditions and experiences. They can be both committed yet open.

Stage 6

Stage 6 is extremely rare. These people seek with everything they have got to reach their ideal. They are visionaries who want to make vision a reality. They are often misunderstood by the very people they try to help. Gandhi and Mother Teresa are two of the examples that Fowler cites.

Activity 4 (I): Stages of faith

I have created three fictional case studies based on Fowler's descriptions of stages 4–6. The age bands given are only approximate.

a. Look at the three case studies, and the description and case study for stage 3 on pages 101–2, then choose one stage and think of someone you know who you think is at that stage.

   ◆ How like Fowler's descriptions are they?
   ◆ How unlike Fowler's descriptions are they?

b. Think about ways in which an awareness of faith development could affect the way you use the Bible in Christian ministry. Look at the parable of the great feast (Luke 14:15–24). How would you use this passage with someone in stage 3? How would your use change for someone in stage 5?

Activity 4 (G)

Photocopy the four descriptions for Fowler's stages 3–6 and the four case studies (include the stage 3 case study and description on pages 101–2). Cut them up, shuffle them and share them out among the group. Ask people to pair up so that each pair has a matching case study and description. After this follow the individual activity.

Stage 4: Any time after late adolescence

Danielle is in her late twenties and has recently brought her own house and started a new job. She is a very reflective person and has thought a lot about her faith, spending time discussing ideas with friends. She has a strong sense of identity as a Christian and is at ease with herself. She does not rely for her identity as a Christian on other people. Danielle has made thoughtful choices about her faith, values and lifestyle and she can give an account of what she believes and why she believes it, though it has taken a lot of struggle to get to this point.

Stage 5: Unusual before mid-life

Jack, 50, was brought up in a Christian home. His faith grew over the years and he was baptized when he was 17. He and his wife are key people in their church. Lately Jack has been through some difficult times: he lost his best friend in a car accident and several of the people he grew up with have died. This has left him feeling vulnerable and aware of the shortness of life. Life and faith seem much more complex to Jack at 50 than at 25. Truth seems less clear-cut, for he has met a wide variety of people and come to recognise the reality of their faith, though different to his own. This does not lessen his personal commitment; rather he feels a deep well of faith, almost a return to the faith of his childhood. This security gives him an openness to the faith of others and humility that he did not have in his youth.

Stage 6: Extremely rare

Luc and Marie gave up lucrative careers in finance and spent twenty years fostering damaged children. They worked closely with the authorities, yet desperately wanted to change the system, so they set up and are running an organisation called Alternative Care, ploughing in all their own money. They still work with the local authority but they offer something different. They give unstintingly of themselves and transform the lives of those around them and they in turn have been changed. Life is not easy for Luc and Marie: their own deep faith has led them to embrace people of all faiths and none as part of their work and this has sometimes led to them being misunderstood. Their vision is wide and few share it, for it is costly.

Feedback

a. I thought about a Christian called Kate in her late twenties. Danielle's description and the stage 4 description fit Kate fairly well. She is unlike Danielle in that she does still rely on others for her identity to some extent. I think people are rarely independent concerning their beliefs. I think there is always a *degree* of dependence on others and that is not a bad thing.

b. If I used the parable of the great feast with someone in stage 3 I would stress the relational aspects of the parable. I might explore the parable from different perspectives: the King, the guests, the servants. I would make a point of bringing out the beliefs and values. If I were working with someone in stage 5 I would create a much more open-ended study and explore how Christian traditions other than my own understand this parable.

Reflection

Exploring faith development models raises a number of issues that are relevant to the use of the Bible in Christian ministry. Look at the following questions and record your thoughts in your reflective diary.

◆ What happens when the majority of the congregation is at a *significantly* lower or higher stage than the leadership?
◆ Do leaders like congregations to stay at certain stages? (They are easier to live with if they do not progress too far!)
◆ Do leaders keep people at a certain level by their use of the Bible? (This is not a likely to be a conscious choice.)
◆ How can you prevent people at a high level being perceived as a threat, particularly by the leadership?

5. Differences in personality

Understanding different temperaments can help us have a better understanding of ourselves and others and impact the way we use the Bible in pastoral practice. Many people are now familiar with the Myers-Briggs classification of personality types based on the earlier work of Carl Jung. For information on this go to www.personality pathways.com and www.typelogic.com. The Myers-Briggs test is not without its critics and a useful article on this test can be found on www.en.wikipedia.org (search by Myers-Briggs then scroll down).

Activity 5 (I/G): Personality type and the Bible

If you are comfortable doing so, go online and take a test to get an indication of your personality type (www.humanmetrics.com). How accurate do you think this is? Please note that these are not the official test: for that there is a charge. In what ways do you think personality can affect the way a person uses the Bible? For groups, people will need to take the test before the session if you have that option.

Feedback

My personality type was ISFJ. I think personality type could be very important in leadership teams. The type of the dominant person could be set up as *the* way of handling the Bible.

6. Differences in learning

There are many different ways of categorising how we learn; one is which sense we predominately use: visual, auditory or kinaesthetic. Most of us have a preferred learning style or styles. This is what we tend to use for *new or difficult* material.

◆ Visual learners like to see words and images and can visualise things in the mind's eye.
◆ Auditory learners like to hear information, enjoy discussion and often hold silent conversations in their minds.
◆ Kinaesthetic learners enjoy the physical and emotional sensations that go with learn-

ing, the 'tingle factor' that many people get when they grasp something new. They also like to learn by doing.

We have tried to use different styles of learning in this book: you might like to flip through a few units and identify the different styles.

Different learning styles will affect how people react to the Bible. For example, insisting that everyone follow a reading in their Bible is not appropriate for those who respond better to listening. Others may prefer to see dramatised Bible readings or have them visually presented with images. This does not mean that people should be restricted to their preferred style or pigeon-holed as a particular type of learner. The important insight to be applied is that we need to employ all three styles and be flexible. The Bible can be presented in a variety of styles *over a period of time*; all three do not have to be used each time the Bible is presented! The research project revealed some creative ways of presenting the Bible; using images, drama, music, oral story-telling, painting and poetry.

Reflection

In many churches the congregation may have an auditory preference because that is what has always been used and people have 'self selected' on that basis (gone somewhere where they are happy with the style). However, people outside the church or on its fringes may have very different learning styles. What possibilities and problems might this present the pastor with when using the Bible with these different groups? Record your thoughts in your reflective diary.

Activity 6 (I/G): Learning styles

Select from the following.

a. Think of times when you have experienced these three styles and give examples. Which did you prefer? What do you think is your preferred style? If possible go online and take an unofficial test to find out your own style at: http://pesdirect.com/lsitest1.html
b. For a month track the different learning styles that are used to present the Bible in your church service (just make a few notes during the service). Sum up how you would describe the balance of learning styles. Are different people catered for?
c. Interview some people in leadership at your church or ask if they are willing to take a test. Do leaders tend to reflect one learning style?

Feedback

I tracked the learning styles used in church, which were largely auditory, though some people put images with their sermons and the Bible reading and some preachers created visual images by their descriptions. The kinaesthetic was least used, particularly the 'doing' aspect which tended to be confined to activities around the text rather than the text itself.

Final reflection

Look back over the unit. What have you learned about yourself through this unit? What two things have you learned about others? What would you like to know more about? Record your thoughts in your reflective diary.

Review

As a result of studying this unit you should now be able to:

◆ describe some differences between people in terms of faith journeys, faith development, learning and personality and how that affects the use of the Bible in ministry.
◆ explain how a person's concept of the 'ideal Christian' may affect their use of the Bible.
◆ begin to develop strategies that will allow you to respond to people in varied ways.

Resources

Astley, J. (1991) *How Faith Grows*. National Society/Church House Publishing.

Astley, J. and Francis, L. (1992) *Christian Perspectives on Faith Development*. Gracewing.

Cooling, M. (2004) *Creating a Learning Church*. Bible Reading Fellowship.

Fowler, J. W. (1981) *Stages of Faith: Psychology of Human Development and the Quest for Meaning*. Harper and Row.

Francis, L. and Robbins, M. (2004) *Personality and the Practice of Ministry*. Grove Books Ltd.

Francis, L. 'Pastors or Mission Leaders?' in *Quadrant*, 24 January 2006.

Jamieson, A. (2002) *A Churchless Faith: Faith Journeys Beyond the Church*. SPCK.

Lyall, D. (2001) *The Integrity of Pastoral Care* (New Library of Pastoral Care). SPCK. Chapter 6.

www.faithmaps.org Select 'Articles' and 'Leadership'.

www.findarticles.com Search by 'Adult faith development' 'faith journeys' and 'Pastoral Care'

www.pastoralreport.com Go to links for a range of sites

www.religion-online.org Select 'Practical theology' and 'Counselling and mental health'

www.acc.uk.org

Section 3

Pastoral Contexts

Unit 9

The Bible in pastoral visiting and listening ministry

Key question
How can I most appropriately use the Bible in the context of pastoral visiting and listening ministry?

Preparation
The option on page 95 involves using magazines.
The option on page 95 involves an interview.

1. Introduction

Pastoral visiting and listening ministry is what comes to mind when most people hear the word 'pastoral'. This ministry can be formal and involve trained professionals or it can be informal and consist of mutual pastoring by members of the congregation. This unit will look at appropriate ways of using the Bible in these situations.

Note: 'Listening ministry' is used here instead of 'counselling' as this is a technical term and applied to those with a specialist training.

The research project showed that the majority of practitioners (over 80 per cent) used the Bible in some way in pastoral contexts. The Bible was often used allusively; it was not necessarily read or directly quoted. Our use of the Bible in pastoral contexts will be influenced by many things, for example, our spirituality and religious tradition. Catholics and Baptists are likely to differ in the way they handle the text as they view biblical authority and tradition in different ways. Another factor governing our Bible use will be how each of us came to be in our present pastoral role and where we find our authority when in that role (unit 3).

Reflection

Look back on your own life and think about how you came to exercise your pastoral role. Is it something you were trained for or did it evolve? Did other people recognise your gifts or were you someone who was just 'there'. What do you feel gives you your authority in that role? Is it your professional training, your gifts, the church, the relationship, the Bible or something else?

2. The relationship between the Bible and training

Those who have a listening ministry in church are often unsure about how they relate the Bible and pastoral ministry. There may be a tension between being person-centred, non-judgemental, and listening – essential characteristics of effective personal ministry – and being Bible-centred, discriminating, and wanting to allow the text to speak. If the Bible is allowed the main voice, the person may be silenced, unheard, or made to feel somehow inadequate. Furthermore, the Bible might be used by a pastoral worker as a kind of shield against really relating to the person.

Can the Bible be part of good practice or is it an 'either or' choice? All of the following people have been on a secular training course in pastoral ministry; they have chosen different ways to integrate their use of the Bible and their training.

---

a. *Wesley searches his Bible for principles, practices and purposes that he can apply in pastoral situations, but he is unhappy about insights from non-biblical sources such as contemporary pastoral practice.*

b. *Sophie likes to use insights from the Bible to* enlighten, guide and inform *what she does but she relies largely on her secular training.*

c. *Jake likes to select biblical themes and images such as Jesus as the good shepherd, and use them in his pastoral ministry* alongside *insights from contemporary pastoral practice.*

d. *Frank tends to use different forms (genres) from the Bible for particular situations. For example, he uses the Psalms when he is working with someone who has been bereaved.*

e. *Alice uses underlying biblical themes such as 'fall and redemption' or 'strength in weakness'. She interprets these in the modern context as part of her contemporary pastoral practice.*

Note: these five case studies draw on the five ways of relating the Bible and pastoral practice listed by Stephen Pattison in *A Critique of Pastoral Care*.

Activity 2 (I): Relating the Bible to pastoral practice

Using a highlighter, mark the case study that is nearest to your own practice (you can highlight more than one). What do you think this says about your view of the Bible in pastoral practice? Sum it up in one sentence.

Activity 2 (G)

As for the individual activity, but enlarge the five descriptions and place them around the room. Ask people to stand under the description they most strongly identify with.

Feedback

I found it difficult to choose. Probably c. and e. describe what I do most closely.
I think this reflects my concern to integrate the Bible in my practice but my unease about using the Bible in ways that would not be seen as good practice in secular pastoral terms.

3. The Bible, pastoral style and the pastoral cycle

Sometimes those engaged in pastoral practice suffer from a vague unease, a sense that the Bible ought to be important in their ministry, but they are unsure of the role it plays. The research project highlighted the formational role of the Bible e.g. the Bible forms the pastor and acts as his or her framework, offering insights, challenge and comfort. Others were more specific in their use of the Bible, sharing readings and quotations. Some did this as a matter of course, others as they felt it was appropriate.

Our role changes with the situation. In some situations it is right to be approachable and act as friend, in other situations, such as funerals, people may need a pastor to be more objective. Whatever the style of the pastor may be, or the situation may demand, the Bible can have an input in pastoral ministry.

The Bible can also have an input at all stages of the pastoral cycle, rather than being 'applied' at one stage. The Bible can form part of experience; it can frame the analysis, reflection and action and shape the celebration. (Go to www.neafe.org, select 'Saltley Trust', scroll down and select 'pastoral cycle' – click on diagram to see a different version of the cycle. See also www.freshexpressions.org.uk, select 'base communities'.)

Activity 3 (I): Pastoral images

Images are often used to communicate the role the 'pastor' adopts. Look through the list of images that follows and highlight those that describe the modes you feel you adopt most often. Use a different colour to highlight images that describe other roles you occasionally adopt. What does your selection tell you about your pastoral style? In what way do you think your image of your role influences the way you used the Bible?

Shepherd	Gardener	Guide
Storyteller	Agent of hope	Intimate stranger
Midwife	Wise fool	Wounded healer
Diagnostician	Ascetic witness	Coach
Moral counsellor		

Activity 3 (G)

Place the different images on paper around the room. Ask people to walk around and add their comments to each. The comments should reflect how that image may influence a pastor's use of the Bible. Use the notes as a basis for discussion. Alternatively, follow the individual activity.

Note: these images draw on Robert Dykstra's lecture 'Who shall we be?' www.pastoralreport.com Search by the title/author.

Feedback

My main role seems to be storyteller and midwife. This leads me to a narrative and open-ended approach to the Bible. I'm not sure what my images tell me, except that I am non-directive.

4. Handling the clashes

At some point in their Christian ministry most people have to handle conflicts between a person who is the recipient of pastoral care and the Bible. There are two main issues:

a. Is the person allowed to question the Bible?
b. What do I do, as 'pastor' when the person's aspirations conflict with the Bible?

Both questions will be affected by the view of the Bible held by the person acting as 'pastor', but there is no simple equation between a person's attitude to the Bible and how they behave in a pastoral situation. Other factors beside the Bible come into play such as personality, style, context, church tradition and training. However, the way a person views the Bible will be influential.

Reflection

Identify an occasion when you experienced a clash between the aspirations of the person you were 'pastoring' and the Bible. How did you react? What factors came into play? Record your thoughts in your reflective diary.

Note. We are aware that the issue of abuse of power is not dealt with here. Go to www.safeinchurch.co.uk.

5. Verses for all occasions

If you go to a hotel you will often find a Bible with a list of verses for particular occasions at the front. Many people have found this helpful; it is self-help and unpressurised. This approach relies on the work of the Holy Spirit without a human agent to be effective. However, some have taken this model and used a similar approach in pastoral situations.

Activity 5 (I): References and relevance

Email the following references to a friend asking them to assess how helpful they would find them. Alternatively, use the group activity.

References:

Facing temptation: Hebrews 2:18; James 1:2–3; Romans 8:37
Facing depression: Isaiah 61:1–3; Psalm 34:15, 17; Romans 8:26–27
Fearful: Psalm 23:4–5; John 14:27; Psalm 91:10–11
Angry: Ephesians 4:26; James 1:19–20; Proverbs 15:1, 18

Activity 5 (G)

Discuss the pros and cons of using verses in this way. Draw some scales on a large sheet of paper and around the scales list the group's suggestions.

Feedback

These are our group's suggestions:

	Pro	**Con**	

Pro

Quick and effective if the verse is appropriate

Easily remembered and repeated during the day

Obvious use of the Bible could be reassuring

Con

More like a prescription than a relationship

The verse may have been meant for a different situation

Could encourage a superficial 'diagnosis' of problems

6. Pastoral visiting

Pastoral visiting is often initiated by the person in the pastoral role, e.g. a hospital visitor or chaplain, though it is sometimes requested by the individual concerned. The recipient enters a pastoral visit with a set of expectations. For example, they might expect the Bible to be used if the person in the pastoring role is clearly a Christian, or they might expect the pastor to listen without talking about God unless asked to do so. They might expect the person doing the visiting to have some training.

In the research project many people thought that pastoral visiting was a sensitive situation for using the Bible. Some people carried a pocket Bible as it was less obtrusive; a few offered a verse at the end of the visit so that people had something to meditate on. It was felt that the use of the Bible in visiting depended on the relationship and there was concern not to exploit the situation.

Activity 6 (I): Using the Bible with integrity in pastoral visiting

Think of a particular pastoral visiting situation e.g. visiting someone in hospital.

a. What might be the hopes of the person being visited concerning the use of the Bible?
b. What might they fear or dread concerning the use of the Bible?
c. What do you think is good practice concerning the use of the Bible in this type of situation?

Activity 6 (G)

Use the individual activity, but the hopes and fears of the person being visited can be enacted using the technique called 'Mind Alley'. To create a 'mind alley' all but one person should form two lines facing each other (as in a barn dance). The lines become the 'mind' of the person being visited. One side represents hopes, the other fears. The person who did not become part of the alley becomes the practitioner who walks down the line. Each person forming the alley should speak one hope or fear appropriate to that situation as the practitioner walks by. Discuss how these hopes and fears can be taken on board and how they might affect the use of the Bible in that situation.

Feedback

I feel that the use of the Bible in situations such as hospital visiting, where people are especially vulnerable, is particularly sensitive. Sometimes the direct use of the Bible can be too intense in such contexts. Christians should not take advantage of people at such moments when a person might already feel overwhelmed. I think it is best to discover whether a person wants prayers or Bible readings by asking them either directly or indirectly. In some cases it might be appropriate to ask what bit of the Bible they think might help, letting them set the agenda so that their needs are uppermost. Using the Bible in this way stops it being seen a something used by people in power on those who are powerless.

> I think some people in hospital may feel embarrassed at having the Bible read in a public place if they are very private about their faith. They may fear a situation developing that they cannot control. They may hope for some comfort and some words that will be meaningful in what is often a frightening situation.

Option: Pastoral protection

Think of a time when you have received a pastoral visit and the use of the Bible has been either awkward, embarrassing or too intense and has made you want to blush. Imagine you could apply a cream to prevent embarrassment and blushing (like sun cream to prevent sunburn). What factor cream would you have needed to apply for that situation? Was it a mere factor 15 or a factor 50? What made the situation embarrassing/too intense? What would have needed to change to make the situation a positive experience?

7. Key Moments: birth, marriage and death

Bible Society research (*The Use of Scripture* June 2000) suggested that the key moments in life are times when the Bible is most often used in pastoral visits. For example, when someone dies the Bible may:

◆ *Create the framework for thinking about the event even if a Bible is not opened.* The pastor may explain that this world is not as God intended, sorrow and sin mar a world that God created good and there is neither sin nor sorrow in heaven (Revelation 21:1–4).
◆ *Suggest attitudes and approaches.* We can weep with those who weep (Romans 12:15) and offer comfort, or sometimes learn to keep silent in the face of suffering (Job).
◆ *Speak for itself as readings in the funeral service or as part of the liturgy.*
◆ *Provide the images that help thought and feeling.* Even if they are not immediately taken up, they can sit in the imagination. For example, death as a wasp with the sting removed (1 Corinthians 15:55).
◆ *Inform rituals.* For example, the practice of throwing some soil into the grave echoes Adam being made from the earth (Genesis 2:7). See unit 12 for more information on rituals.

Activity 7 (I): Creative use of the Bible at key moments

Take either birth or marriage as your focus and create a collage by cutting pictures from magazines or using clip art from the computer. Leave gaps between the images and, in the gaps, suggest ways the Bible can creatively input into the situation. Alternatively, describe a creative way of using the Bible in marriage or baptism.

Activity 7 (G)

As for the individual activity, but make a group collage on a large sheet of paper.

Option: Interview

Interview a couple who have been through a 'key moment' recently and ask them how the Bible was used with them at this time. How helpful did they find that use?

Feedback

I interviewed a couple who had been recently been married. Toni and Mike had lived together for two years before they got married and they attended marriage classes for several months run by a member of the congregation who was trained as a counsellor. I felt from the way Mike and Toni described the situation that the Bible set the framework, as people were accepting and open, reflecting the words from John 3:17 that Jesus came to save not to judge. Toni had been afraid they would be criticised because she and Mike had been living together. The Bible was also used creatively in looking at subjects such as handling disagreements.

Final reflection

Look at the key question: how would you answer it in light of this unit? In what ways could insights from this unit enrich your use of the Bible in pastoral visiting, your listening ministry or your involvement in key moments in life? Record your thoughts in your reflective diary.

Review

As a result of studying this unit you should now be able to:

◆ explain some ways in which the Bible and contemporary practice in pastoral ministry may relate.
◆ describe different images for the role of pastor and how they may affect Bible use.
◆ give examples of how the Bible can be used sensitively in pastoral visiting, listening ministry and at key moments in life in creative and positive ways.

Resources

Atkinson, D. and Field D. (eds) (1995) *New Dictionary of Christian Ethics and Pastoral Theology.* Inter-Varsity Press.

Ballard, P. and Pritchard J. (1996) *Practical Theology in Action: Christian Thinking in the Service of Church and Society.* SPCK.

Capps, D. (2003) *Biblical Approaches to Pastoral Counseling.* Westminster John Knox Press

Carr, W. (1985) *Brief Encounters,* London, SPCK.

Challis, W. (1997) *The Word of Life: Using the Bible in Pastoral Care.* Marshall Pickering.

Clinebell, H. (1984) *Basic Types of Pastoral Care and Counselling,* SCM.

Lyall, D. (2001) *The Integrity of Pastoral Care* (New Library of Pastoral Care). SPCK.

Pattison, S. (2000) *A Critique of Pastoral Care* (third edition). SCM.

Peterson, E. H. (1980) *Five Smooth Stones for Pastoral Work.* Wm. B. Eerdmans Publishing Co.

Wimberly, E. (1994) *Using Scripture in Pastoral Counselling.* Abingdon Press.

Woodward, J. and Pattison. S. (eds.) (2000) *The Blackwell Reader in Pastoral and Practical Theology.* Blackwell Publishing Ltd. Chapter 16.

www.acc.uk.org

www.findarticles.com search by 'Pastoral care' using free articles

www.pastoralreport.com go to links for a range of sites

www.religion-online.org Select 'Practical theology', 'community' and 'Counselling and mental health'

www.schoolofministry.ac.nz see pastoral subjects

Unit 10

Pastoral issues in using the Bible with children

Key question

What issues need to be addressed if my use of the Bible with children and young people is to be appropriate?

Preparation

Some of this unit may need doing in a local bookshop or library unless you have access to children's books at home.

There is an option for an interview on page 101.

1. Introduction

As we grow and develop in faith our understanding of the Bible develops and changes. Understanding how children develop in faith can help us to use the Bible appropriately with them in a range of pastoral contexts.

The Bible is not a child's book (it's not a book the average adult would pick off the shelf either). The research project showed an awareness that what a story or teaching conveys to an adult and what it conveys to a child might be very different. For example, the story of Abraham's near-sacrifice of Isaac is not likely to be an encouraging story for a child. The Bible contains stories of a violent and sexual nature and has teaching that baffles adults. Despite this we continue to use it with children because it also contains a wealth of material that is relevant and captivating and deals with the big issues of life. However, when we use the Bible with children questions concerning appropriateness need to be asked.

How a child responds to the Bible will be affected by their life experience, background and stage of development. These developmental and background issues need to be borne in mind when selecting Bible material. They will also affect the amount of explanation and background information we may have to give.

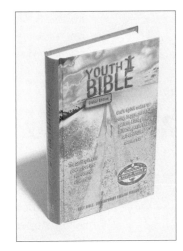

Activity 1 (I): A suitable book for children?

a. Think back to your own childhood: did you ever read or hear a Bible story or text that frightened, worried or just confused you? Can you think of a Bible story you would be reluctant to use with children?

b. Visit a local book shop, library or use children books from around the house if you have them. Browse through children's story books, and DVDs looking at the *content*. Do they have things in them that might scare, worry or confuse children? (Look at both traditional tales and modern stories.) If secular children's literature contains things that frighten or confuse, what are the implications for our use of parts of the Bible that might be frightening or difficult?

c. Look at the *style* and *presentation* of secular books and DVDs for children and compare them with the way Bible story books and DVDs are presented. Do Bible story books and DVDs look as if they might be attractive to children?

Activity 1 (G)

As for the individual activity but either meet in the bookshop or library or ask people to bring a selection of books marketed for children.

Option: Biblical computer games

Imagine the stories of the Bible being turned into DVDs or computer games. Think of one story that would be rated as suitable for young children, one suitable for mid-teens (15 plus) and one for adults only. You might like to think of titles of parallel secular DVD/games that would be in the same bracket, e.g. your Bible story for young children might relate to a Walt Disney title.

Feedback

a. I remember thinking how worrying it was when Samuel was lying in his bed and God could get in and speak to him in the middle of the night. I think I also found this intriguing, especially the bit about him not recognising the difference between God's voice and Eli's voice. How could he fail to notice the difference?

   I would be reluctant to use the story of Noah with very young children.

b. Lots of secular children's books seem to have scary things in, but often (though not always) it comes from the evil characters. I think this means that we do not have to avoid everything frightening. *The problem with the Bible is that some of the scary stuff comes from God*; he seems to command death and destruction. This puts Bible stories into a different category. I don't think scary is always wrong; it depends on the framework within which it occurs.

c. At one level I was pleasantly surprised by the Bible story books for children. A lot of care seems to have been expended at the level of presentation and style sometimes making an effort to fit in with recognisable secular models. For example Andy Robb's *Boring Bible* echoes the *Horrible History* series. The content, in contrast, does not fit with other material that young people read. Secular literature for older children does show an interest in the paranormal, but not traditional religion.

2. Pastorally unsuitable stories

As you may have concluded from the activity in the previous section, parts of the Bible are sometimes judged as inappropriate for children today. Previous cultures may have been less squeamish and some people think that we may be unduly protective of children, underestimating what they can understand. Children also *may* have ways of grasping stories and dealing with difficulties that does not necessarily depend on the development of rational thought.

The problems children encounter with the Bible is similar to those experienced by adults. Both have problems interpreting the text (unit 5) and for adults and children certain texts create pastoral problems (unit 6). However, adults have abilities of interpretation and understanding that children do not. This does not mean that all sensitive stories are omitted. It does mean that there are stories that we probably would not want turned into computer games for children to play! A number of strategies are often employed with pastorally sensitive stories:

IT'S A RANGE OF BIBLE-BASED VIDEO GAMES. HIS FAVOURITES ARE "DESTROY SODOM", "SUPER EVANGELIST BROTHERS" AND "ARMAGEDDON 2 - RETURN OF THE BEAST"

©hris Morgan 2002   cxmedia.com

a. Tell part of the story, not the whole, stopping before a sensitive part. For example, stop the story of Jericho before the massacre.
b. Tone down the language.
c. Omit detail.
d. Paraphrase the story to make the language and concepts easier to understand.
e. Omit some stories entirely.
f. Supply background information to help children understand the story in context.
g. Balance the stories and put the difficult story in the context of the bigger biblical picture.
h. Allow lots of time for questions and discussion with appropriate age groups.

Activity 2 (I): Pastorally sensitive strategies

a. Look at Bible story books for children and work out what strategies the writers use with pastorally sensitive stories. (See feedback for ideas of things to look for.) Add any other strategies you use or have seen used.
b. Which strategies do you tend to adopt?
c. Are there any potential problems with using these strategies?

Activity 2 (G)

Share your ideas concerning strategies and create a table of strategies used and potential problems on the flip chart.

Feedback

a. I found most of the strategies used except g. and h.
b. I tend to use a. b. and c. most often.
c. I think that by omitting parts of the story I am in danger of violating the text and I sometimes wonder if I cut bits out because I do not want to handle awkward questions rather than out of sensitivity to the needs of the children. I think I would still omit parts of some stories but I need to make sure that these stories are progressively filled in as the children grow older. I also think that it is important to discuss tough questions about how God is portrayed in some stories, so that children gain a maturing understanding of the nature of God. Too often a haphazard selection of stories are told, just because they are 'traditional' without regard to the picture of God that might be developing in children's minds.

Reflection

People can become stuck in childhood ways of understanding biblical stories and not progress. You may have encountered this. How could you actively encourage people to keep retuning to biblical stories at different stages of their lives and reconsider how they view them? Record your thoughts in your reflective diary.

3. Faith development and the Bible

Most of us are aware that our faith has changed over the years. In order to be pastorally sensitive in our use of the Bible we need to consider where children and young people might be in their faith journey and how this might affect their understanding of the Bible. James Fowler, an American researcher, described a series of stages of faith, three of which apply to children (pages 101–2). Fowler views the stages as progressive: children move from one to the other and the order does not vary. Movement between stages is often triggered by new or challenging experiences. One of the most helpful insights to come from Fowler's work is that movement between stages can be both exciting and unsettling. This period of movement can lead to questioning which parents and leaders may find difficult to cope with. But, if Fowler is right, questioning can be a sign of a child or teenager developing in faith rather than losing their faith. The ages given for the stages that follow are only loose guidelines – some adults remain at stage 3 all their life. For fuller descriptions of these stages go to:

> www.jmm.aaa.net.au/articles/2219.htm
> www.facaulty.plts.edu/gpence/html/flowler.htm
> www.en.wikipedia.org/wiki/Stages_of_faith_development
> www.reality.org.nz/articles/33/33-pritchard.asp

Stage 1: 3–4 to 7–8 years

At this stage the imagination is made up of a collection of powerful images and life tends to be a series of episodes and impressions rather than a developed story. The child's ability to reason is limited and thinking is likely to be intuitive. Cause and effect is only partially understood and adopting another person's perspective is difficult. God is not always pictured as human and may be imagined in non-human form e.g. as air or light. Authority figures are adults and faith is picked up by imitation. Faith is shaped by experience and formed in trusting relationships. Moral decisions tend to be based on rewards and punishments. At this age children respond well to symbols but they are something to be experienced rather than explained.

Stage 2: 6–7 to about 11–12 years

At this stage thinking develops and thoughts become more ordered as control is exercised over the imagination. Cause and effect are beginning to be mastered but abstract thinking is difficult. Story is very important in building an understanding of life, particularly the story of the community to which a child belongs, for there is a strong sense of belonging. Children at this age can see some things from another person's point of view, particularly if the people are like them. Symbols are interpreted more literally than before and God is more likely to be described as having human characteristics. Fairness and justice become important to children in this stage but they find reflecting on their thoughts and feelings difficult.

Stage 3: 11–12 to about 17–18 years (some adults remain in this stage)

At this stage young people can think abstractly, reflect on their thoughts and actions and see things from different perspectives. Relationships are important, particularly relationships with the peer group and with significant people in their lives. Teenagers are not always clear about what they believe and their beliefs and values may be drawn from a number of places. God is not imagined with human features and symbols are not separated from their meaning. Moral thinking is often about living up to the expectations of significant others.

Note: Fowler's work has come under criticism, for example, not all agree that there is an upward, hierarchical movement. See the bibliography.

Activity 3 (I): Ages and stages

The three case studies that follow are fictional and have been created using Fowler's descriptions. Read all three then select one and think of a child/teenager you know that is of similar age. Either interview the parents or reflect on your own knowledge of that child/teenager and answer the following questions:

a. How closely does the case study reflect your experience of that age group?
b. In what ways do you think the stage description is inaccurate?
c. Write down one or two ways in which an understanding of faith development might affect your use of the Bible with children of that age.

Activity 3 (G)

As for the individual activity, but share your responses to the age profiles and discuss rather than write.

Stage 1

Kieran is five. His world is largely made up of his family although it is beginning to widen out as he has started school. His parents, and now his teacher, are his authority figures. He is constantly coming home and telling the family what his teacher says. Kieran has a strong faith largely nurtured by his family and developed within the trusting relationships of home. He also has a strong sense of right and wrong which has been encouraged and informed by his parents. Kieran's imagination is a riot of images and he tends to find it difficult to follow a logical argument. He is learning about cause and effect and this is getting easier as he grows. Kieran does not find it easy to see things from other people's point of view but this too is developing as he grows older. Kieran likes symbols and rituals: he loves the ritual of circle time at school and the colour and symbols at church. When his teacher asked him to draw God he drew a big sun but many of his friends drew God as a big man.

Stage 2

Emma is nine, and she is in junior school. Her favourite things are computer games and dancing which she does on a Saturday. Emma's favourite time at school is when she is free to read stories by herself. Fairness and justice are extremely important to her as she has a strong sense of right and wrong. Emma believes in God but would find putting her faith into words difficult. Emma's faith, unlike Kieran's, was not developed at home but was put together piecemeal from a number of sources. Friends and family are important to her; she has a strong sense of belonging to her family, her school and her clubs. Emma finds reasoning easier than Kieran and she has a better understanding of cause and effect. Her imagination is also more controlled and she can see things from other people's point of view if the people are like her. She interprets symbols literally, unlike Kieran who experiences them rather than interprets them. When the teacher asked Emma to draw God she drew a big man.

Stage 3

Aisha is sixteen. She has a strong group of friends at school and at church and these, and a few key adults, are the major influences in her life. Aisha is very concerned about green issues and animal welfare. She wants to live up to certain ideals, particularly those of people she respects and admires. She can think abstractly and can see things from other people's perspective. Her beliefs and values are a bit of a patchwork and Aisha is not really sure of what she believes but she has a strong relationship with God whom she does not see as a 'big man' as she did when she was younger. Aisha enjoys symbols and rituals at church and they have meaning for her but she does not separate the meaning and the ritual. Belonging to a Christian community is important for Aisha; she is beginning to take responsibility in church.

Feedback

a. My grandson is Kieran's age and this is reasonably accurate concerning his limited reasoning ability, the way he responds to symbols and his sense of right and wrong.
b. I think my grandson has more of an understanding of cause and effect than Fowler allows for, and more ability to empathise. I'm not sure he only imitates, there seems to be something much deeper going on.
c. This will affect my choice of material and the response I expect, though the child's background will come into play as well.

4. Spirituality, children and young people

Religious faith and spirituality is not the same thing, for a person can have a deep spirituality but it may not be informed by religious faith. Traditional religion may not be popular with the young but that does not mean that they are not spiritual in any way. There is a strong interest in the spiritual – however vague that may be – and this can be encouraged and celebrated as well as channelled and informed. Researchers such as David Hay and Rebecca Nye suggest that the childhood years (pre-teen) are the peak time of spiritual awareness. We need ways of using the Bible that tap into this spirituality and inform and develop it. Hay and Nye's research indicates that the core of children's spirituality lies in:

◆ an unusual level of consciousness (a heightened awareness).

◆ an awareness of the relatedness of things: how I relate to myself, to others, the world, God.

There seem to be a range of triggers for spiritual experiences both positive and negative. They include:

◆ natural beauty
◆ prayer and meditation
◆ sacred places
◆ the creative arts
◆ depression, distress and despair
◆ illness and death

Being aware of these triggers means that we can integrate them into our use of the Bible with young people. We can use the creative arts (unit 15) to explore appropriate passages. We can create biblically-based prayers and meditation exercises or read biblical passages while showing images of natural beauty. Incorporating *appropriate* negative triggers needs sensitive handling but these subjects do not have to be avoided with children and young people, as that would deprive them of the Bible's message of hope. However, it is important to judge the right age and stage for these subjects. Going into hospital might be appropriate for young children, but not depression.

Reflection

Go to the Alister Hardy website (www.alisterhardytrust.org.uk) and read some of the spiritual experiences there. They may trigger some memories of your own spirituality as a child. If they do, make a note of your memories. Select one appropriate trigger from the list above and think of ways in which this might influence how you use the Bible with children and young people. Record your thoughts in your reflective diary.

Activity 4 (I/G): Using the Bible to inform spirituality

Design or describe a session for either children or young people that will draw on and inform their spirituality using the Bible. Look at the feedback for an example.

Feedback

Our Pathfinder group used Micah 7:19 and a variety of other biblical passages to explore some of the Bible's teaching on forgiveness. They used role play to work out how it might be applied, evaluating and refining the role play. Each person was given a pebble and they wrote the word 'sin' on it in water-based felt pen. Time was spent mediating on the verse from Micah while music played and people held their pebbles. The pebbles were then dropped it in a plastic bowl of water as a reminder of the verse from Micah.

Final Reflection

Return to the key question and consider your response. Now think of what you have explored in this unit; try to think of your study as opening presents rather than collecting information. In light of this metaphor, what gift would you say this unit has given you? Record your thoughts in your reflective diary.

Review

As a result of studying this unit you should now be able to:

◆ articulate your understanding of pastoral issues that arise when using the Bible with children.

◆ explain how issues of faith development can inform the use of the Bible with children.

◆ suggest ways of using the Bible that takes into account the spirituality of children.

Resources

Astley, J. (1991) *How Faith Grows*. National Society/Church House Publishing.

Astley, J. and Francis, L. (1992) *Christian Perspectives on Faith Development: A Reader*. Wm. B. Eerdmans Publishing Company.

Bridger, F. (2001) *Children Finding Faith* (revised edition). Scripture Union/CPAS.

Coles, R. (1991) *The Spiritual Life of Children*. Houghton Mifflin.

Fowler, J. (1981) *Stages of Faith: Psychology of Human Development and the Quest for Meaning*. Harper and Row.

Francis, L. and Kay, W. (2002) *Children, Churches and Christian Learning*. SPCK.

Farnell, A. et al. (2002) *Opening Windows: Spiritual Development in the Primary School*. The Stapleford Centre.

Hay, D. and Nye, R. (2006) *The Spirit of the Child* (revised edition). Jessica Kingsley Publishers.

Saunders, C. and Porritt, H. (2004) *Working with 8–10s*. Scripture Union.

Westerhoff III, J. (2000) *Will our Children Have Faith?* (revised edition). Morehouse Group.

Williams, T. and Stephenson, J. (2004) *Working with 11–14s*. Scripture Union.

www.findarticles.com search by 'The Bible and children' and 'Faith development' and 'Teenage attitudes to God' using free articles

www.childspirituality.org

www.immanuelprinceton.org/youth/stages

www.evangelism.uk.net select 'Children and youth'.

www.religion-online.org Select 'Local Church Education' or select 'Evangelism'

Unit 11

The Bible and small groups

Key question

How can my use of the Bible with small groups be more creative?

Preparation

You may need a church magazine or notice sheet for the activity on page 106, though they are not essential.

1. Introduction

The rise of 'cell churches', 'emerging churches' and the continuing significance of small groups in church life makes the issue of how groups function important. The research project reflected this, although the purpose of small groups varied from denomination to denomination. Participants were engaged in a range of small groups from church housegroups to contextual Bible study in prison. The size of small groups means that they can function pastorally at an informal level as everyone is known to each other and there is time to get to know each others' concerns. How the Bible is handled in small groups needs careful reflection, for small groups can frustrate as well as encourage the pastoral and creative use of the Bible.

Reflection

Think about some of the small groups to which you belong. Ponder the following:

◆ why do you belong?
◆ what keeps you going?
◆ what do you give to the group?
◆ what do you receive?

Record your thoughts in your reflective diary.

2. Purposes

Small groups meet for different purposes and this will affect how the Bible is used or indeed whether it is used at all. The purpose of a group needs to be clear as the leaders may have one purpose in mind and the members of the group another. For example, the leaders may think Bible study is the main purpose while the group think that pastoral care is more important.

Activity 2 (I): Primary purposes

a. Divide a piece of paper into two vertical columns.
b. Use a church magazine/notice sheet or draw on your memory to write a list of small groups that operate in your church in the first column.
c. In the second column copy the list of purposes that follow. You can add ideas of your own.
d. Identify the main purpose of each group. You can do this in any way e.g. by high-lighting, arrows, etc.
e. Choose one group from your list and note its main purpose by drawing an arrow, then highlight any other functions it fulfils. Is its official purpose its core activity in practice?

List of purposes

a. To be church
b. Prayer
c. Worship
d. Care and support
e. To spur one another to love and good deeds
f. To encourage one another
g. Evangelism/mission
h. Bible study
i. Discipleship
j. Social interaction/fellowship

Think about the way the Bible is used in the group that you have selected; does the purpose of the group match the way the Bible is used? For example, if the main purpose of the group is fellowship, the Bible might be used in a different way to a group whose main purpose is study. There might be more of an emphasis on people sharing passages from the Bible than on focused Bible study. On consideration, does this group need to change its name, function or the way it uses the Bible?

Activity 2 (G)

Follow the individual activity, but do the diagram on a large sheet of paper.

Feedback

These are my two diagrams.

I was about to give up leading my housegroup as I did not think I had enough biblical knowledge. Looking at the list, I reconsidered what the group was for and decided that in practice it is not really a Bible study group. This gave me a different perspective so I have decided to carry on.

3. The nature of groups

The dynamics of small groups is complex and there is not room to explore this subject in detail here. Instead we have focused on two common situations. For more information on group dynamics go to www.mapnp.org/library/grp_skll/theory/theory.htm or www.smallgroups.com (some material is free).

Experiences of groups can be mixed. Some create an environment which encourages people to explore the Bible and its relevance to life. Others are stilted or dull and leave people frustrated. Relationships within the group can either aid the exploration of the Bible or frustrate it. Sometimes it is difficult to work out what is causing the problem as various factors influence group behaviour:

◆ how long the group has been together.
◆ the stage the group is at.
◆ seating arrangements.
◆ attitudes and personalities.
◆ the roles people adopt.
◆ attitudes to power, authority and leadership.
◆ the style of leadership.

Groups can also be affected by numbers. The ideal number for a small group is debated; 5, 8, 10, 12 and 15 are numbers often quoted. When creating small groups, factors such as age, interests, where people live, and stage of faith (e.g. basics groups) also have to be considered.

> *Magda sighed and sank back into the sofa; she seldom volunteered her opinions on a text or asked a question as she was very shy. Magda had not been a Christian very long and there were many things she wanted to ask about the Bible but all the rest of the group seemed to know so much. She was frightened of saying something that would make her feel stupid.*
>
> *Steve gritted his teeth; Isobel was doing it again, using such super-spiritual language that to differ from her made you look less spiritual. Every time Isobel did this the discussion of the Bible died away, no one challenged her as they all feared it would lead to an argument – all dressed up in religious language of course.*

Activity 3 (I/G): Developing strategies

Look at the case studies and say what you would do to improve relationships so that the Bible could be studied more effectively by everyone.

Alternatively, say how you would organise housegroups or Bible study groups in your church (e.g. neighbourhood, work-related, shared interest, faith stage) and give reasons for your choice.

Feedback

In the case of Magda, I would spend time getting to know her in other social contexts so that she began to feel more relaxed. I would also ask her to respond by talking to the person next to her so that she only had to speak to one other person rather than to the whole group.

Note: for information on dealing with 'Isobel' and other small group matters go to www.intervarsity.org, search by 'Small groups' and locate the article 'Taming the Over-talkative'. See also page 113.

4. Cell churches

The terms 'cell church' and 'emerging church' describe a range of Christian initiatives where people form congregations (often small group congregations) that are tailored to fit local needs. They might be based on a need or a shared interest or they may grow out of existing provisions such as a mother and toddler group. This is the opposite of a 'one size fits all' church. It allows worshipping communities to spring up and function in ways that suit them. This builds on the insight that in modern cultures people often belong before they believe; they might join a group – often an informal one – and believing might grow, rather than belonging *because* they believe. See the information at the end of this unit for details on these two movements. For more information go to www.celluk.org.uk and www.emergingchurch.info.

Activity 4 (I/G): Developing 'church'

Look at the case study and think of a way in which the Bible could be used in that situation that would be appropriate for the group.

Joel works at his local leisure centre; he is well known and has developed good relation-ships with many local people. Joel has started a men's group aimed at clients who want to change to a healthier lifestyle by getting fitter and changing their eating habits. Joel wondered whether he could add a spiritual dimension to this lifestyle class, a sort of spiritual health check, as an option.

Feedback

I think that Joel could start with a voluntary lifestyle questionnaire and a short optional session picking up on the results of the survey. Some biblical insights into spiritual life could be shared, for example, the need for rest and 'Sabbath time' and the idea of abundant life. He could see how it grew from there.

5. Different ways of thinking

If we wish to make creative use of the Bible in small groups, we need to consider the different ways in which people think in order to design material that will be fit for its purpose.

Convergent

Convergent thinking works from information towards one answer or solution. A Bible study based on this type of thinking might involve looking at the text and discussing

pre-written questions leading to an answer that is usually found in the text and then applied to life. The emphasis tends to be on communicating biblical knowledge. If this is your main purpose, then conver-gent questions will help to do this. A convergent question on the feeding of the five thousand would be: 'What was Jesus' response to the disciples' concern about the hunger of the crowd?' This arrow diagram would represent convergent thinking.

Divergent

A divergent way of thinking works from information outwards to see possible con-sequences and applications. Divergent thinking explores a range of possible 'answers'. Questions will tend to be open-ended and the group will be encouraged to think out

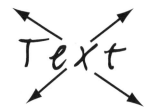

from the text. The emphasis tends to be on meaning and application rather than acquiring information. If this is your main purpose, then divergent questions will help you achieve this. A divergent question on the feeding of the five thousand might be: 'Why do you think Jesus responded in the way he did to the disciples concern about the hunger of the crowd?' This diagram represents divergent thinking.

Reflection

Sometimes Bible studies will be a mixture of these approaches; sometimes they will be one or the other. Look at the case study examples that follow. Do you think they are convergent, divergent or mixed? Which do you prefer? Record your thoughts in your reflective diary.

Activity 5 (I): Exploring the text in different ways

Look at the case studies that follow, giving examples of three approaches to Bible study. Select one or more of the following activities:

a. Choose one case study. You might wish to read it, then close your eyes and imagine what it would be like to experience that approach. Write a diary entry for someone who has attended that Bible study, recording their reactions.
b. Evaluate the three approaches as a way of using the text. Also bear in mind the pastoral possibilities of each approach as you assess them. You could create a table or some other method of showing your results.
c. Look at the Bible study material your group uses; do you think it is convergent, divergent or somewhere in between? Which of the case studies do you think it is closest to? To what extent does the style of the Bible study material make mutual pastoral ministry easier? To what extent might it hinder mutual ministry?
d. Write your own Bible study material using one of the approaches; you might want to try the same passage in various styles. If possible, ask others to use it and evaluate it.

Activity 5 (G)

Either choose one of the individual activities, or try out one of the three approaches and critique it.

Case study 1: A questions approach]
Read Genesis 15. (Background information would need to be supplied.)

Introduction
As you listen to the reading, try to listen with fresh ears. What do you find surprising, interesting or puzzling?

Initial activity
On post-it notes, write questions that you, as a group, want to ask about the text and anything you find confusing or unclear. Place the post-it notes on a large piece of paper and arrange them into two groups:

Group A
Questions that are straightforward to answer using the text and background information.

Group B
Questions that cannot be answered directly from the text or background information and need more careful thought.

Core activity
Answer group A questions as quickly as possible and remove them from the paper. Take the group B post-it notes and arrange these into themes, e.g. questions about God, questions about behaviour. Use these to guide your discussion.

Case Study 2: An integrated application approach
Read Genesis 15.

a. Look at the way in which God describes himself in verse 1. Why do you think God chose these images at this moment in Abraham's life? Would these images fit your experience of God? What words/images do you use of God? Why?

b. Read how God introduces himself to Abraham in verse 7. If God were to introduce himself to you, how do you think he would do it? What events in your life would he cite?

c. Abraham's faith in God's promises goes up and down in this chapter. Read it through and, as a group, draw the ups and downs as a temperature chart. What affects the faith of Abraham? When does his faith tend to plummet? When does it rise? Can you see a pattern emerging?

d. Think about the way in which you respond to God's promises and compare your responses with Abraham's. Can knowing our pattern of response and what affects it help us? As a group, explore what it is that makes our faith plummet and what raises it. What can we do when we feel our faith plummeting?

Case study 3: A 'from text to life' approach
Read Genesis 15.

Introduction
◆ Think about promises you have been made. Have people kept them?
◆ Think about promises you have made to others. Have you always kept them?
◆ What sometimes stops us keeping our promises?

Looking at the passage
This passage is about promises God made to Abraham.
◆ How does God describe himself to Abraham (vv. 1, 7)
◆ What promises does God make? (vv. 4–18)
◆ What is Abraham's response? (vv. 2, 6, 8). Have you seen people react like this?
◆ What is your impression of Abraham from this passage?
◆ What can we learn from this passage about our own response to God's promises?

 Feedback

I think our Bible study material is nearest case study 3. It can be very good but the questions tend to be a bit obvious as they are very convergent and don't always stimulate discussion.

6. Different approaches to using the Bible in small groups

The small group provides the opportunity for using a range of approaches. The ones that follow are those suggested by the United Bible Societies (see resources).

◆ *Meditation.* This is spending time with the Bible, allowing the words and images to sink in and their meaning to become part of us. In meditation our needs and the Bible text come together.

◆ *Transposition.* This involves changing the form in which the Bible is expressed. For example a text can be changed into a poster, a prayer, a poem or a song. The process of changing the form can help in exploring the message.

◆ *Improvisation.* Dramatising the text to help us become part of it.

◆ *Imagination.* This involves using imaginative ways of presenting the text, for example, dramatic readings, presentations with images or reading to suitable background music.

◆ *Interrogation.* Encouraging people to ask questions of the text so that it interacts with their own lives. For example: is this an example we should be following or is this a warning of behaviour to avoid?

◆ *Interaction.* this starts from an issue relevant to the group and then moves to the text, for example, peer pressure and Psalm 1.

Another model for exploring the Bible is to use a parallel text of some form. A parallel text is a reflective text based on a passage and placed alongside it to stimulate thought and to help people to reflect. The research project showed that some practitioners like to experiment with language, writing creative texts for others that help people to engage spiritually and emotionally with the Bible. Creative texts are produced by the Iona community (see www.iona.org.uk, select 'resource group', then 'liturgy').

The parallel text that follows is based on Matthew 14 and Matthew 3:1–3 and draws together the death of John the Baptist and the feeding of the five thousand.

The Duel

A miracle of caring,
but behind the compassion a challenge,
the beginning of a duel.

'Look what the power of a king can do,' said Herod.
'I can prison the Voice of God.'

'Look what the power of the King of Kings can do,' said Jesus.
'I can heal their sick.'

'Look what the power of a king can do,' said Herod.
'I can chain the Voice of God.'

'Look what the power of the King of Kings can do,' said Jesus.
'I can satisfy their hunger.'

'Look what the power of a king can do,' said Herod.
'I can silence the Voice of God crying in the wilderness.'

'Look what the power of the King of Kings can do,' said Jesus.
'I am the Voice of God and He is not silent.'

Both biblical texts and the parallel text would be read by the group and this might be followed by questions.

◆ Can the biblical text legitimately be viewed as a challenge or duel as suggested in the parallel text?

◆ What insights does this way of viewing the text bring?
◆ In what way could our lifestyle challenge others? How may it fail to challenge?
◆ How do we use power?
◆ How far are we the voice of God crying in the wilderness of our own world?

Activity 6 (I/G): Session planning

Plan a session for a small group. Write what you will do as a series of notes and bullet points. You can draw on anything from section 6. For each activity say how it will help people to engage with the Bible. For an example see the feedback.

Feedback

Session for a small group:

a. Start with reading Psalms 22 and 23 from the *Dramatised Bible* to help people to become involved with the text.

b. Move to asking questions of the text, which encourages the group to bring their own concerns. This should make sure the study remains relevant. Example:

◆ Why does the tone change between the psalms?
◆ Are both an example of faith?

Spend time meditating on the text; the different psalms might be read over contrasting music. This may help integrate the text with worship and facilitate the emotional engagement with it.

Final reflection

Look at the key question again and consider your answer. What has excited you about small groups? Has anything in this unit made you concerned? What hopes and expectations has this unit raised? Record your thoughts in your reflective diary.

Review

As a result of studying this unit you should now be able to:

◆ describe some of the roles and purposes of small groups.
◆ explain how some ways in which a group operates can either impede or facilitate the use of the Bible.
◆ give examples of different approaches to small group Bible study.

Resources

Briars, S. and M. (2006) *Homegroups: The Authentic Guide*. Authentic.

Meyer, R. C. (2004) *One Anothering* Vol. 1: *Biblical Building Blocks for Small Groups*. Augsburg Books.

Moynagh, M. (2004) *emergingchurch.intro*. Monarch.

Paul, I. (2004) *Refreshing Bible Study*. Grove Books Ltd.

Perry, M. (ed.) (2004) *A Comprehensive Dramatised Bible*. Collins.
Spriggs, D. (2002) *Feasting on God's Word*. Bible Reading Fellowship.
Warren, R. (2006) *Bible Study Methods*. Zondervan.
Weber, H. R. (1995) *The Book that Reads Me*. World Council of Churches.
Wink, W. (1989) Transforming Bible Study. Abingdon Press.

www.communication-strategy.net Click on 'articles' then select the following: *From First to Twenty-First: the Bible Societies and Scriptural Engagement*.
www.religion-online.org Search by 'Small groups'
www.buildingsmallgroups.com
www.tyndale.org/TSJ/9/russell.html An article on contextual Bible study
www.managmenthelp.org Select 'Index' then 'Group Skills'
www.smallgroupministries.org
www.corpus.org Search by 'small group'
www.christianitytoday.com

Unit 12

The Bible in public worship and personal devotion

Key question
How might the Bible be a more enriching, shaping influence in public worship and personal devotion?

Preparation
◆ This unit includes an option to use a meditative approach to the Bible as part of daily devotion; you might like to try this before the session but this is not essential (page 123).

◆ There is an option of listening to a Sunday service and taking notes (page 119). This can be done before or after studying this unit.

◆ The activity on page 121 involves critiquing devotional material. Websites are provided but if you want to critique book or audio forms you will need to obtain these.

1. Introduction

This unit will look at our most public and communal use of the Bible and our most private and individual use. You will explore different ways in which the Bible can be used in worship, preaching, liturgy, ritual and private devotion. We start by looking at preaching. Many people do not associate preaching with pastoral ministry, but this section will explore how they may relate.

Activity 1 (I): Word association

Draw two overlapping circles (see feedback). Write words that you associate with preaching in one circle and words that you associate with pastoral care in the other. Leave the overlap blank.

Activity 1 (G)

As for the individual activity, but draw the diagram on a large sheet of paper or create circles on the floor from string and place post-it notes with words on inside the circles.

2. Preaching and pastoral care

Preaching and pastoral care are frequently viewed as demanding different gifts. Pastoral care may be perceived as individual and involving non-judgmental listening; preaching may be seen as communal, authoritarian, moralistic and judgmental. These labels and this division of roles are largely a modern phenomenon. Jesus combined both roles; he comforted people and called them to repent.

Preaching and pastoral care are closely related. Pastoral care establishes the relationships into which the preacher speaks. It earths and informs preaching, while preaching shapes the context in which pastoral relationships occur.

Preaching is not just pastoral care writ large.

♦ Preaching often starts with the situations of ordinary people, the situations pastoral care addresses.

♦ Preaching can be a public form of pastoral care, providing the raw material by which people, with God's help, become their own counsellors.

♦ Preaching, like pastoral care, can address sin and sorrow and help to present people perfect in Christ. This is the heart of the definition of pastoral care used in this book (page 36).

♦ Preaching can stimulate spiritual growth, inform, encourage and inspire Christian work and witness and provide the framework in which pastoral care takes place.

♦ Preaching can inform pastoral practice and pastoral encounters can give the preacher access to a wide variety of human experience. This relationship gives preaching depth, demonstrating that the preacher is aware of life's joys and sorrows and can relate these to the biblical text.

Reflection

Is there a case for reversing the roles sometimes? Could preaching to be a context for support and encouragement and pastoral care be a place of challenge and exhortation? If the latter only takes place in the general context of preaching does it make it easy to avoid the challenge? Record your thoughts in your reflective diary.

Activity 2 (I/G): The overlap

Go back to your diagram. Look at both circles. If there are any words that are duplicated or share the same meaning, draw an arrow into the overlap. You may wish to add new words to the overlap that you think both pastoral care and preaching share.

Feedback

Here are my word associations.

Preaching   Pastoral Care

Proclaiming   Listening
Forth-telling   Empathising
    Challenging → ← Asking questions
Teaching guiding —→   Challenging questions
Proclaiming   →   Coming alongside
Comforting —   suffering with/
    Getting people   compassion
        to think   Comforting
Moving to deeper   Guiding
    faith

3. Preaching, the Bible and pastoral care

The selection of biblical texts for worship and preaching can be determined in a number of ways. Some churches use a formal lectionary, others create their own schemes on a short or long-term basis. It's often assumed that a church making its own selection of biblical material is likely to produce more pastorally-orientated preaching than using a lectionary or similar system, as the selection is determined by the needs of the congregation. However, it can also mean that a congregation travels along well-worn grooves and is not challenged – an important pastoral function. If the readings are only selected to meet the pastoral needs of the congregation, the Bible is restricted *by* those needs rather than the text speaking *to* those needs. How the Bible is used within the sermon also varies; no single method or type of preaching is 'pastoral' to the exclusion of other methods.

Activity 3 (I): Preaching styles and pastoral practice

Draw a series of horizontal lines on a sheet of paper as illustrated in the feedback. Look at the following styles of sermon (there are many more). In each case evaluate how effective this style will be as a pastoral tool. Make a mark on each line to indicate your evaluation. Also make a few notes on the use of the Bible in this style. Select the one to which you gave the highest evaluation and explain your assessment.

a. Expository preaching (verse by verse)
b. Imaginative sermons (creative, often using images)
c. Narrative or storytelling sermons
d. Evangelistic sermons (with the emphasis on mission and salvation)
e. Conversational sermons (a conversation between the preacher and the congregation)
f. Devotional sermons (with an emphasis on spiritual life)
g. Topical sermons (covering different topics)
h. Pastoral sermons (with pastoral care uppermost)

Activity 3 (G)

Do the same activity together using a large sheet of paper and discuss your evaluations.

Feedback

Here are some of my evaluations:

a. High——————————————-/———————————Low

   Expository preaching is very methodical on the use of the Bible but there may be many ideas in one passage and not all may be dealt with adequately.

b. High—————-/————————————————Low

   Creative use of images from a passage can help unlock a number of biblical passages as they are often recurring in the Bible, but it only works with certain types of biblical material.

I have given sermons that use images from the text a high score as I think the images they create in the mind can sit in the imagination and develop. Images connect thinking and feeling and this has to be achieved if sermons are to help people pastorally.

4. The use of the Bible in preaching, liturgy and worship

The pattern of a service can provide the context in which the Bible can perform a pastoral role. It can challenge and disturb, comfort and console. In most denominations the Bible has moulded the words of the liturgy, the hymns, the songs and the prayers. Biblical events are also celebrated in sacrament and festival. Liturgical worship and charismatic worship encourage response by the congregation, adding their 'Amens' and 'Alleluias' to worship shaped by the Bible.

In worship Christians come together as part of the worldwide Christian communion and provide a public context for reading the Bible. The regular reading of the Bible reminds people of the story of God's relationship with humanity and restates the Christian vision of how things ought to be. This puts individual problems into perspective and gives people a way of understanding them. In worship, the Bible is experienced in a more objective and communal context which can stop people using it in a way that *only* focuses on their needs. The research project showed that the Bible was still considered important in worship, being reflected in liturgy, hymns, reading and preaching.

Activity 4 (I/G): Tracking the Bible

Choose two or three of the following.

a. During a service note how and when the Bible is used. Look for the way the Bible shapes liturgy, song, prayer, sacrament and other aspects of worship in your church. Find a way of tracking the use of the Bible that suits your situation.
b. Interview some church members; do they think the use of the Bible in church has declined over the years or has its use just changed?
c. Consider your results, are there any ways in which the role of the Bible in worship could be enhanced?

Groups: compare notes after the service.

Alternative

Listen to a sermon and record how you think the Bible and sermon related. A few possibilities are listed below. Add other relationships if you wish to:
The Bible may be reflected in the sermon in:

◆ content.
◆ meaning
◆ structure and style (narrative passages may lead to narrative sermons, the sequence and style of the passage may determine the sermon in other ways).
◆ imagery.

The Bible may:

◆ be mirrored in the sermon (almost a restating).
◆ be echoed or the sermon may resonate with the text (create the same/similar thoughts and feelings but using a variety of means).
◆ act as a framework.
◆ be used to authenticate the sermon which may or may not be related to the text
◆ act as a springboard for the preacher's own thoughts, which may or may not relate to the text.

Question:
Are the sermons with the most obvious use of the Bible the most biblical?

Rev. Ted had mixed
feelings about the new
sermon evaluation
committee.

Feedback

This is my record of a service. Looking at it, I think we could allow more time for reflection so that people have time to draw their own conclusions from the words.

Prayer	Liturgy/worship	Sermon/homily	Music/song	Sacrament/other
Opening prayer consisted of words from the Bible.	OT and NT readings. People followed the reading in the pew Bibles.	Text taken from the New Testament and referred to by the lay preacher.	Many hymns had themes and references to the Bible. First hymn was based on Psalm 148.	Communion liturgy: words and actions taken from Scripture.

5. The Bible and rituals

Windridge Community Church had a small but strong young people's group. Some of the older teenagers had just taken A levels; others were moving away with work. The minister did not feel it was right for them to leave without an appropriate goodbye. Together the group, the youth leaders and the minister created a goodbye ceremony which was to be part of the whole church worship. A large board was displayed at the front of the church and one by one the young people came and placed their photograph on the board with a short summary of where they would be and a yellow wrist band with their name on it.

Over the previous months various scriptures had been chosen and studied as a source of encouragement as the teenagers moved from the familiar setting of home into new challenges. During the service various members of the congregation read these scriptures. A CD was created for each person with the verses of scriptures, encouraging messages from the congregation and photos. After the CDs were presented, various people came and prayed with the young people, placing hands on their heads to bless them.

The congregation were asked to choose a young person to 'adopt'. They did this by removing a yellow band at the end of the service. With the 'adoption' came a promise to pray and send either letters or postcards to help the young people over the first few months of settling in to their new lives. There was also a commitment to look after these same people when they returned in vacations as that is a time when students are often neglected. After the service there was coffee and cake and time for people to chat.

Our need for rituals is sometimes underplayed; hearing the Word is not enough, we need to do something to bring the meaning home. Through rituals meaning can be experienced rather than analysed, for rituals compress large amounts of meaning into dramatised action. The physical act of going through a ritual can help people to come to terms with a situation or express a feeling or understanding. Rituals are usually something a group or community do together, creating a common bond, but biblically meaningful rituals can be created for individuals or whole churches. Many people have lost the rituals associated with the rites of passage that once marked the stages of life such as baptism and marriage; as a result, many look for rituals in new spiritualities.

Activity 5 (I/G): Creating biblically informed rituals

Look at the following situations and choose one. Design a ritual that will use the Bible or draw on the text in some way.

- ◆ A 'friends' day, where the bonds of friendship are celebrated.
- ◆ A celebration for the arrival of long-term foster children.
- ◆ A grandparents' day
- ◆ A ritual for parents whose children have left home.

Feedback

I chose 'Friends day'. I would start by sharing readings that demonstrate different aspects of friendship: David and Jonathan (closeness, like-mindedness), Martha, Mary and Lazarus (hospitality), the early Christians: Acts 2:43–47(fellowship) and John 15:9–17 (acceptance).

We would form a circle/s and pray for each other by putting names (photos) in a hat and pulling them out, then praying for that person and 'toasting' them.

We would share times of quiet and music together.

We would end with sharing food and fun.

6. The Bible and personal devotion

The Bible can act as 'pastor' at a personal level. Bible Society research (*The Use of Scripture,* June 2000) showed that personal Bible reading was encouraged publicly by the majority of leaders (84 per cent). Only 2 per cent of respondents said that personal Bible reading was not encouraged. Some Christians like to cover the whole Bible in a set time, for example by reading through the Bible in a year. Some follow a theme or explore a biblical book in depth. Some people use meditative practices as an aid to their devotional use of the Bible, with the text being the focus for prayer, thought and contemplation. Others prefer a different type of study where they work out what the text is saying using techniques such as colour coding, key words, creating lists and looking for patterns. People's preference for the form of Bible they use also varies: some people use online devotions, others use the Bible in book form, CD or audio. Some people have texts and comments delivered by email or to their phone.

Reflection

Do you have one favoured approach to the Bible in personal devotion or do you adopt a range of approaches? Which approaches would you recommend to other Christians? Which aids would you want to discourage, why? Record your thoughts in your reflective diary.

Activity 6 (I): Critiquing devotional material

Choose one piece of devotional material to critique. It can be in book, audio or electronic form. Write a brief response to each of the following:

a. Is the aim of the material clear?
b. Is it an appropriate aim?
c. Does it fulfil that aim?
d. What would be the experience of the person using that material?
e. Does the material respect the integrity of the text?
f. What are its pastoral possibilities?
g. How could it be improved?

Activity 6 (G)

As for the individual activity, but share your responses to the material. The evaluation of the study and sharing responses can be done on the day if the material is in book or audio form. If you use an internet site, people may need to look at this before the meeting if you do not have access to a data projector.

Useful websites

www.grow-with-the-bible.org.uk Click on free sample

www.rejesus.co.uk/spirituality/daily_prayer

www.creighton.edu Click on 'ministry' then 'daily reflections'

www.dailybible.com Click on a version, then on a date, then select

www.biblesociety.org.uk select 'Church and community' then 'Faith comes by hearing' then 'Experience faith comes by hearing', choose from the selection of audio clips

www.su-international.org go to 'Explore the Bible' then 'Way to read or listen to the Bible'

www.word-on-the-web.co.uk Select 'Bible studies'

www.gospelcom.net Click on 'devotionals'

www.everydaywithjesus.com/docs/search.asp Click on free samples

www.rbc.org/utmost

www.purposedrivenlife.com Click on one year plan

www.taize.fr/en Select 'sources of faith' then daily reading and meditation

Feedback

I looked at *Word for Today*.

a. The aim of the material was clear, which is to provide daily readings and reflections.

b. The aim was appropriate.

c. It sometimes fulfilled the aim but as there were a lot of authors and themes, it depends if you 'click' with the author.

d. How a person responds would depend on how thoughtful they are.

e. Normally the material respects the integrity of the text. Sometimes the response to the text is very creative.

f. Pastorally it was good and non-threatening.

g. I'm not sure how it could be improved.

7. Meditative practices

There are a range of meditative approaches to the Bible which can form part of a persons' devotional use of the Bible. This section looks at two popular approaches.

An Ignatian approach

This involves a person choosing a scene from a passage and imagining themselves as part of it. All the senses are used to engage with the scene. Questions are asked such as 'Which character do you identify with?' 'What feelings resonate with you?' Sometimes a person might want to speak to a character in the scene and they might spend time thinking about what they would say to that character and how the character would reply. For more information go to www.spiritualorientations.com and select 'helps for personal prayer'.

The Lectio Divina approach

This is a form of spiritual reading that involves 'listening with the heart'. There are three stages:

1. *Reading/listening.* This is slow quiet reading and 'listening' with plenty of pauses to allow words to sink in and a period of waiting for God's Spirit to speak.
2. Once the reader has found something that speaks to them personally, the words are pondered and relished. The words of the Bible are allowed to interact with a person's hopes, experiences and thoughts.
3. Finally prayer is offered to God. This is conversational prayer where thoughts, hopes and experiences are given to God and God's Word takes on a transforming role.

For more information go to www.valyermo.com/ld-art.html

Activity 7 (I): Evaluating devotional practices

Choose one of the forms of meditation to try yourself. It can be done on a passage of your choice. After you have tried one meditation write a brief response to the following questions:

a. how far do these approaches free the Bible to be a shaping influence?
b. how helpful are they in comparison with a study-based approach?
c. how do you stop these approaches being too comfortable?
d. how do you stop these approaches being scary if someone goes somewhere in a meditation that is not healthy?
e. how do you stop inappropriate connections being made?
f. how pastoral are these approaches?

Activity 7 (G)

As for the individual activity but comment as a group rather than writing. Alternatively, try one of the forms of meditation as a group.

Feedback

a. Scripture can focus a period of meditation but if the passages are personal choices there might be a danger of one's preoccupations and prejudices colouring a meditation. Can a new view be found alone or do we need the trigger of other people's words and thoughts?
b. Bible study material can give you a more immediate end result in the sense of more immediate ideas.
c.–e. I think group meditation with guidance is one of the ways of overcoming some of these problems, or using a spiritual director. Alone, people can wander into unhelpful places.
f. I think these approaches could have a strong pastoral role as the focus is on personal interaction with the text.

Final reflection

Go back to the key question. How would you answer it? What aspect of this unit have you enjoyed most? What aspects would you want to share with others in your church? Record your thoughts in your reflective diary.

Review

As a result of studying this unit you should now be able to:

◆ articulate your own understanding of how the Bible can function as part of public worship and ritual.
◆ describe and evaluate some meditative approaches to the Bible.
◆ describe and critique personal biblical devotional material.

Resources

Alling, R. and Schlafer, D. (2005) *Preaching as Pastoral Caring: Sermons that Work* XIII. Morehouse.

Ballard, P. and Holmes, S. R. (eds) (2005) *The Bible in Pastoral Practice*. Darton, Longman and Todd. Essays 13,14 and 16.

Bowe, B. E. (2003) *Biblical Foundations of Spirituality*. Rowan and Littlefield Publishers Inc.

Capps, D. (2003) *Pastoral Care and Preaching*. Westminster John Knox

Challis, W. (1997) *The Word of Life: Using the Bible in Pastoral Care*. Marshall Pickering Chapters 2 and 3.

Goldingay, J. (2002) *An Ignatian Approach to Reading the Old Testament*. Grove Books Ltd.

Leach, J. (2005) *How to use Symbol and Action in Worship*. Grove Books Ltd.

O'Connell Killen, P. and De Beer, J. (2004) *The Art of Theological Reflection*. Crossroad.

Oliver, G. (2006). *Holy Bible, Human Bible: Questions Pastoral Practice Must Ask*. Darton, Longman and Todd.

Ramshaw, E. (1987) *Ritual and Pastoral Care*. Fortress Press.

www.religion-online.org Select 'The art of preaching'
www.lectionary.org
www.rejesus.co.uk Select 'Spirituality'
www.brf.org Select 'Foundations 21'
www.textweek.com

Unit 13

The Bible and the unchurched

Key question
What factors do I need to bear in mind when using the Bible with the unchurched?

Preparation
Groups: you will need a cardboard box and a butterfly pin for the optional activity on page 126.

You will need access to a TV and possibly a TV guide for the option on page 128.

1. Introduction

People who are outside the church context (the unchurched) may still encounter the Bible in other settings, as described in the case study that follows. Sometimes this will be a positive experience; at other times we may feel it breaks all the rules of good practice. It is important to consider when people may have encountered the Bible being used as this may form their attitudes when people use the Bible with them in the future.

> *The preacher stood in the market square beneath a large sign that proclaimed God's anger with humanity. He held a Bible aloft and shouted in a monotone to passers-by about God's judgement. Every sentence was prefaced by the words: 'The Word of God says ...' His preaching did not seem to be directed at anyone in particular and he never made eye contact. Shoppers either put their heads down and hurried by or smiled at the sight of this sad person.*

Activity 1 (I): Discomfort and delight

Think about an occasion when you experienced the Bible being used outside church. Draw a 'cringeometer' and mark on it where you would have the arrow pointing to indicate how you felt. (A cringeometer is an imaginary machine that measures embarrassment levels.)

Try to work out what has caused the arrow to swing, and make a note of any principles of good practice that you think your example either demonstrates or violates (page 21).

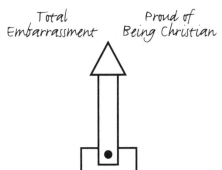

Activity 1 (G)

As for the individual activity, but make a cringeometer by fixing a card arrow on the side of a box with a butterfly pin. Ask people to share experiences and move the arrow to show how they felt. Alternatively, draw the cringeometer on a large sheet of paper. You may want to vote on who has described the most cringe-generating experience.

Feedback

I witnessed a TV debate where one speaker kept referring back to the Bible. There seemed to be no acknowledgement that this book held no authority for the audience. There was no attempt to relate what the Bible said to anything the audience might understand. This incident had a medium cringe factor as it demonstrated a total lack of awareness.

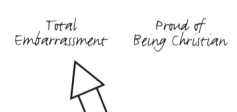

Reflection

Think about your own use of the Bible with the unchurched. In what ways does it differ from your use of the Bible in a church/Christian context? Record your thoughts in your reflective diary.

2. The gulf between the church and the 'unchurched'

People outside the church rightly see the Bible as a book from an alien culture; it comes from another time and may have little to do with their lives. If we don't take account of this we may use the Bible in inappropriate ways in the community. On the other hand, we can become so aware of the difficulties it can lead to paralysis. The research project revealed a reluctance to use the Bible overtly with non-Christians; people tended not to produce a physical Bible for fear of creating barriers. However, some people spend their lives ministering outside the church, for example, chaplains in hospitals, prisons, industry and schools. These people can rarely assume faith where they work and have to adapt the way in which they use the Bible.

Reflection

Could the problem be with the churched rather than the unchurched? People inside the church have got used to the Bible and it no longer feels alien. Could those outside the church bring fresh understandings of the Bible to those inside the church? Record your thoughts in your reflective diary.

Activity 2 (I/G): Problems and possibilities

Jot down all the difficulties that might prevent the Bible being used with the 'unchurched', putting each difficulty on a separate slip of paper or post-it note. Once you have a number of slips of papers, sort them into groups. For example, one group might relate to the language of the Bible. Choose one group and suggest one strategy that might lessen the difficulty.

OH! I FORGOT TO MENTION THE CULTURAL GAP YOU HAVE TO LEAP

©hris Morgan 1995   cxmedia.com

Feedback

I came up with the following difficulties:

a. difficult language.
b. difficult ideas.
c. 'unacceptable' behaviour of people and God in stories.
d. 'holy' nature of book makes people reluctant to engage with it.
e. lack of skill in distilling what the Bible is really saying.
f. preconceptions e.g. that the Bible is only for religious people, it is irrelevant to others, it's the Church's book and not for the 'unchurched'. (It was written largely for believers.)
g. lack of skill in presenting the Bible to people who do not go to church.
h. negative media images.
i. negative associations, particularly with the Bible as a source of authority and power.
j. lack of skill in discerning where people are and what is going on in their lives.
k. concentrating on communicating biblical information rather than touching people's lives.

I think that e., g. and possibly j. are possibly a set, with the common element being that they all reflect a lack of skill on the part of the user. One strategy could be some skills-based training in these three areas: g. is often taught, but the others are sometimes missed.

Reflection

The Bible was primarily written for those of faith: Israel, the early church. How far can we use it outside this context? Record your thoughts in your reflective diary.

3. Communicating with the unchurched

If we are concerned to use the Bible with unchurched people then we have to take modern cultures seriously and bear in mind how information is presented and processed. The research project showed some awareness of changes but the degree of the changes and the possible consequences for the use of the Bible in pastoral practice are seldom fully appreciated.

Here are some of the ways in which information is presented to people today:

a. Lots of ideas are dealt with in story form e.g. soap operas.
b. It is fast moving, often with frequent changes.
c. Information is conveyed visually rather than by the spoken or written word.
d. It is often acquired in a relaxed setting: cinema, TV, home computer.
e. It is often something people do alone and it *can* be passive – see f. (Modern youth do not emphasis *formal* belonging; groups are fluid.)
f. Interactive learning is increasing with interactive TV, the web and computer games.
g. There is preference for experience and emotion over concerns about 'truth'.
h. There is sometimes a low level of intellectual demand: learning is often intuitive.
i. Information may be presented in non-sequential form and have gaps.

Activity 3 (I/G): Changing patterns of learning

Watch TV for about 20 minutes, flipping between channels and sampling as many programmes as possible. Include some adverts. As you watch, make a mark against any of the points (a.-i.) above when you come across an example of them in your viewing. Consider the following and note your response:

a. Do your impressions resonate with the suggestions about the way in which learning has changed?
b. What do these changes in learning suggest about our use of the Bible?
c. Which of the points do you think are positive?
d. Which are negative?
e. Should our use of the Bible conform to these or be 'counter-cultural'?

Feedback

a. I felt that much of the list was confirmed but there seemed to be a tension: people wanted experience and emotion but they seemed to be getting it second-hand, through technology.
b. I think this has consequences for my desire to make our use of the Bible relational and experienced based *as well as* imparting information.
c.–d. I think aspects of b., e., g., h. and i. are negative as it could lead to a downward spiral in thinking. For example if we keep lowering the demand or preferring emotion over truth the losses could be greater than the gains. The others could be positive and there are also positive aspects of e. and g.
e. I do not think we have to go along with all of this; it might be where we start, but not where we finish.

4. Different models of using the Bible with the unchurched

Various organisations are exploring ways of using the Bible with the unchurched and relating faith to contemporary cultures. Four organisations describe their work here. Further information can be gained from their websites.

Case Study 1: RUN www.run.org.uk

RUN is an interdenominational network of hundreds of churches from across the UK and beyond who are united by the common passion to reach people for Christ in a culture that has largely given up on the church. It is committed to resourcing, envisioning and networking without promoting any one single model of practice. RUN encourages churches to engage creatively with those beyond their normal reach and is committed to telling stories of what people are finding helpful in mission. One of the most effective ways we have found is to use the Bible in a multi-media context as with our 'in motion' DVD. Here we use clips of the actor Rob Lacey performing the 'Word on the Street' in locations such as a shopping mall, the top of a bus and in a restaurant. We have also produced a database of drama sketches specifically written with the unchurched in mind. These demonstrate the power of story and are a highly effective means of communicating biblical truths within everyday contexts.

Case Study 2: AGORA www.agoraspace.org

Agora aims to create new opportunities for people to talk together about the issues of living in today's world. It is committed to the idea that faith perspectives and the Bible have a place in these conversations and has been exploring different ways of presenting the Bible. One important strand has been the recognition that all human societies need to work with narrative in their search for wisdom. So we have explored presenting Bible as story in conversations on subjects such as immigration, building trust in a mobile society and religion and violence. The Bible is often 'told' in a semi-dramatic form while remaining faithful to the text. We tell some of the difficult stories as well as the nice ones. We particularly like to work with diverse groups of people in secular venues like pubs and cafes and to work in an interactive style that helps everyone participate.

Case Study 3: DAMARIS www.damaris.org

Damaris is committed to rigorous study and effective communication as it seeks to relate biblical Christian faith and contemporary popular culture. This is carried out as follows.

Biblical study

Damaris has great respect for the Bible and believes that it is God's word. Damaris engages in rigorous study of the Bible's content and context in order to understand and respond to it with integrity.

Cultural study

Damaris has great respect for contemporary popular culture and believes that it is an expression of people's search for answers to fundamental questions. Damaris engages in rigorous study of its content and context in order to identify, understand and respond to the underlying worldviews with integrity. >>

Biblical communication
Damaris has great respect for people and their freedom, and acts as a humble guide to the Bible. Damaris invites people to consider and respond to the message of the Bible, including the answers it provides to questions raised by popular culture.

Cultural communication
Damaris has great respect for people and their freedom, and acts as a humble guide to contemporary popular culture. Damaris invites people to evaluate and respond to the underlying worldviews.

Case Study 4: REEL ISSUES www.reelissues.org.uk

Aims and description
Bible Society's Reel Issues *service aims to enable Christians and others to relate the Bible to the stories and values in popular films and to their lives. It seeks firstly to resource groups (ideally outwardly-focused with a mix of Christians and others) and secondly to resource preachers.*

Every month subscribers download from the web a set of discussion materials for a film newly released on DVD and can access a bank of all previous discussions. The materials include a film synopsis, identify themes in the film and explore these through suggested clips with open questions and 'God's Story', a Bible briefing with further questions on these issues. Research has found that 48 per cent of users use the materials in groups and 35 per cent use the materials to illustrate talks and sermons.

Principles
Reel Issues *takes its cues from the themes within films so that it actively addresses the concerns and aspirations voiced in popular culture and that influence us and our peers. It invites group members to say how they view these themes and then to discuss together how Bible narrative and teaching addresses them. It assumes belief on the part of leaders but not of members.*

Reflection

Read the case studies and think about the principles each is using to make the use of the Bible relevant to modern cultures. What do they share in common? Record your thoughts in your reflective diary.

Activity 4 (I/G): Using the Bible without alienating people

Design an evening that 'unchurched' people could be invited to. How could the Bible be used during the evening in a way that will not alienate the people attending? For ideas consult the Damaris, Run, Reel Issues or Agora websites.

Feedback

I would plan a 'recognition' evening where the church celebrated what was going on in the local community and thanked people. Short bits of the Bible that were positive and reflected the work of these people could be used. People's work could be recognised with 'awards' followed by a thank you buffet from the church.

5. The Alpha course

Alpha is a ten-week introduction to the Christian faith devised for people who would like to explore the spiritual questions of life in a relaxed way. People can come for only one session or stay for all ten. Each evening follows a pattern of meal, worship, video/talk and discussion. The groups ideally meet in a home but often meet in a church hall depending on numbers. Group leaders use their Bibles, though open Bibles may be less evident for the first few weeks so as not to intimidate people. Guests are also encouraged to use Bibles, looking up quotations used in the talks. Issues raised in the video are discussed in small groups with the group leader asking questions to stimulate discussion. The tone is neither argumentative or judgemental. If an answer to a question is not known, leaders are encouraged to say they do not know and to seek an answer which they report at a later occasion. Lots of details and comments on Alpha can be found on the website www.alpha.org.uk.

> *Alex felt a bit out of place. He had never been to anything like this before but several of his friends had been to an Alpha course so he signed up. He was welcomed at the door and the evening started with a meal. People seemed friendly enough and no one was pushy or waved a Bible at him.*
>
> *After the meal there was some worship which Alex was very unsure about and a talk by the minister that showed how the Bible related to life. The talk was informal, interesting and relevant. Alex hadn't expected it to be like this; his image of religion was that is was dull, boring and useless.*
>
> *After coffee they got into groups and discussed some of the things the minister had said. Although he was told he could ask any question, Alex felt reluctant to participate, but many members of the group did ask questions and the leaders did not seem to mind, even if the questions were hostile. Throughout the discussion the group leader referred to the Bible and related it to the questions the members put to her.*
>
> *Alex was left wondering. This group did not fit the image of Christians he had picked up from the soaps. He decided to go the following week and maybe ask some questions himself.*

Activity 5 (I/G): How Bible-friendly and pastoral is Alpha?

How far would you say that Alpha is pastoral in its use of the Bible with the unchurched? You might like to revisit Stephen Pattison's definition on page 36 and draw on what you have read, the website and your own experience. If possible, interview someone who attended an Alpha course about their experience. What did they find helpful/unhelpful concerning the way in which the Bible was used?

Feedback

I think this use of the Bible could be pastoral in the sense that it allows people to ask questions about important issues in a relaxed setting. I think Alpha is more evangelistic than pastoral. This is fine, as that is its aim, but group leaders could be so intent on making people become Christians *by this particular route* that they miss the questions people are really asking and the problems they really want to share. The use of the Bible could be too focused in this regard.

6. Essence

We live in an age that *feels* very secular and there *appears* to be a lack of interest in traditional religion; but many people are interested in spirituality (however vague that might be) and some turn to New Age spiritualities. Various initiatives help churches to engage with the spirituality of those outside the Church. For resources with practical ideas go to www.ChurchinaSpiritualAge.org.uk. Essence is an initiative which offers a spirituality drawn from the Christian tradition and uses the Bible in this context. It is designed to introduce people to Christian spirituality, not necessarily to bring them to faith. It is meant to be used in non-church contexts such as pubs, leisure centres or libraries and it is for those who would not go to a church event. A short description of Essence can be found on www.robfrost.org (go to resources).

Libby did not know what to expect when she went along to her first session of Essence. She and her mates had only signed up for a laugh, though they were all interested in spiritual things, and often went to Mind–Body–Spirit shows. The course was held in a room above the local pub and they sat around on beanbags by candlelight with music playing. There was food (bread and dips) followed by an introductory activity so that people got to know each other. Each person was given a piece of string and the pieces were tied together to form a circle to show that people belonged together. Libby giggled, feeling a bit self-conscious, but she joined in the discussion on belonging.

Next there was a meditation involving stones and everyone was given a pebble to take home to personalise. Libby decided to paint hers deep purple. There followed a meditation on a Bible passage (Psalm 23) that was played on CD. Libby recognised a few phrases, but she had not known they came from the Bible. The leader talked about God being like a shepherd who went with us on the journey through life but we needed to listen to his voice amongst the many voices that clamour for our attention.

The evening ended with an activity that involved people threading different beads onto a string to represent important moments in their life. Libby threaded her beads, then laid them on the floor to represent the ups and downs of her life. Looking at the line she felt suddenly overwhelmed. Was that it, her life so far?

Activity 6 (I/G): How Bible-friendly and pastoral is Essence?

Look at the case study.

a. What are your immediate reactions? Record them in a list of bullet points.

b. Try to imagine what it would be like to experience Essence.

c. In what ways could this use of the Bible be described as pastoral? How does it compare with the way the Bible is used in Alpha?

Feedback

a. Reactions:

 ◆ friendly/personal.
 ◆ relevant.
 ◆ quite 'light'.
 ◆ would appeal to people into 'spirituality'.

b. Experience:
 ◆ could be embarrassing or engaging – depends on your personality.
 ◆ could touch the emotions and be relevant.
 ◆ some people might experience it as intrusive. For others this could be a freeing experience.

c. Bible use:
 ◆ The Bible is used in a way that is experience-orientated and designed to touch the emotions and this might open up pastoral possibilities.
 ◆ It uses ways of knowing other than the logical-rational. Alpha tends to work on a more traditional apologetic model and uses discussion. I'm not sure that one is inherently more pastoral than the other; it would depend on your personality.

Final reflection

Re-read the key question and consider your answer. Think through what you have covered in this unit. What one recommendation would you take to your church leadership concerning this subject? Record your thoughts in your reflective diary.

Review

As a result of studying this unit you should now be able to:

 ◆ articulate some difficulties there may be in using the Bible with the unchurched.
 ◆ describe the way in which material is presented in modern cultures.
 ◆ identify ways in which various organisations and initiatives use the Bible in relating to modern cultures.

Resources

Cray, Graham, et al. (2004) *Mission-Shaped Church*. Church House Publishing.
Finney, J. (2004) *Emerging Evangelism*. Darton, Longman and Todd.
Frost, R. (2002) *Essence*. Kingsway Communications Ltd.
Hollinghurst, S. (2005) *Equipping your Church in a Spiritual Age*. Group for Evangelism.
Hunt, S. (2004) *The Alpha Enterprise: Evangelism in a Post-Christian Era*. Ashgate.

Moynagh, M. (2001) *Changing World, Changing Church*. Monarch.

Murray, S. (2004) *Post-Christendom: Church and Mission in a Strange New World*. Authentic Media.

Smith, D. (2000) *Crying in the Wilderness: Evangelism and Mission in Today's Culture*. Paternoster Press.

Stoddard, C. and Cuthbert, N. (2006) *Churches on the Edge: Principles and Real Life Stories of 21st Century Mission*. Authentic.

www.christianityexplored.com
www.dicipleshipexplored.com A follow-on course
www.christianmedia.co.uk Select 'Y course'
www.evangelism.uk.net
www.allsouls.org A source of *Christianity Explored* material
www.iona.org.uk For resources that incorporate Celtic spirituality
www.taize.fr/en Select the resources section for music and prayers

Unit 14

The Bible in work and school

Key question

How can the Bible be used appropriately at work and in school?

1. Introduction

The workplace and schools can both seem a hostile environment for the Bible, but both can also be a fruitful place where the Bible can have a creative input. The recent phenomena of 'workplace church' breaks down the work/worship divide and opens up many new possibilities, as does the increasing numbers of faith-based schools. This unit explores some of the issues around using the Bible in these contexts.

THIS HAPPENED EVERY TIME MARGARET LEFT HER FAITH AT HOME!

For worker-priests or industrial chaplains the secular workplace is their sphere of service. For most members of the congregation work is where they spend a large part of their time and energy and could be their main sphere of Christian ministry. For information and ideas on taking your faith to work go to www.licc.org.uk and select 'WorkWise'.

The Bible might be seen as reinforcing a negative view of work; after all, God worked for six days and rested on the seventh – it is the rest day that is regarded as holy, not the six working days. Work is seen as the result of Adam's sin and Jesus called his disciples from their work to follow him. On the other hand, in the Bible God is depicted as a worker in creating and sustaining the world. Adam and Eve work in the garden before the Fall. Fruits of work were offered to God (tithes) and Jesus worked as a carpenter for most of his life. Work is often (but not always) spoken of positively in the Bible as something to be enjoyed which gives people the means to support themselves and their family. For those who are able to choose their work, it can be a way of expressing their talents.

Activity 1 (I/G): Attitudes to work

Think about your own attitude to work. Which of the following people are you closest to? If you do not feel that any of the characters reflects your attitude, create another character. Record your thoughts in your reflective diary.

a. Les does not particularly enjoy his work. The real focus of his life is his family and leisure activities that work supports.

b. For Cathy, a career is central to her identity: she feels it is her calling in life.

c. Work also figures large for John, but this is because he fears losing his job.

d. Work is something that Rosie enjoys and it gives her enough money to support herself and frees her to work in the church at evenings and weekends.

Feedback

I had to write a new character – Josie. Work is significant for her but so are her family and leisure. She has a sense of calling and wants a career but her career is not central.

2. The role of the Bible at work

Using the Bible in the workplace does not necessarily mean taking in a physical Bible or finding explicit quotes. The Bible can act by transforming elements of the workplace through:

◆ values
◆ attitudes
◆ lifestyle
◆ relationships
◆ ways of thinking
◆ leadership
◆ structure
◆ the way the core task is done
◆ service

Activity 2 (I/G): Transforming the workplace

Choose one of the above and think about a workplace you know. In what ways could the Bible transform it? Give a practical example.

Feedback

I chose service as I work as a receptionist in a doctor's surgery. I pray for the patients and try to show people that they matter by the way that I treat them, bearing in mind the Bible's teaching about each person mattering to God.

3. Unhelpful attitudes

Work is sometimes presented as a spiritual battleground, a place where secularism reigns and which Christians are called to 'infiltrate'. Although there is some truth in this, the use of a military metaphor can be unhelpful for it makes work seem a negative place and one's colleagues become agents of the enemy. Pastorally this can be very destructive. Another unhelpful attitude is to perceive one's role at work largely in terms of evangelism, a means to an end, rather than something valuable in its own right. A third unhelpful attitude is valuing church work, but not secular employment, as service for God, as in the case study below.

Frank could not believe it. His vicar had asked him to fill in a form concerning his Christian ministry. He wrote that he was head of the church secondary school in the parish and sent it in. The form had just come back to him with a note saying that this was not what they were looking for: could he please list what he did as church work? Once Frank had calmed down he decided just to add a note saying, 'as before' and leave it at that.

The Bible contains some positive attitudes to work that are not pastorally destructive. Each can act as a model.

♦ Joseph and Daniel both worked for the secular state and received praise just for being good at their job. They both worked in pagan environments, yet they transformed them. God was with them and blessed them because they did their *core task* well (Colossians 3:17).
♦ Esther had little choice about her role but used the power and influence it gave her for good. She accepted the responsibility that the little power she had brought.
♦ Bezalel and his team are described as having God-given talents that they expressed through work (Exodus 31:1–6).

Activity 3 (I/G): Biblical models for the workplace

Think of your own work in terms of the three biblical models above. What insights could each bring? See the feedback for an example.

Feedback

a. Daniel and Joseph: I could go on training courses in order to do my work better.
b. Esther: I could identify what power I have and explore how I can use it responsibly as a Christian.
c. Bezalel: I could see how my gifts could be expressed through work.

4. The Bible in school

All of the material in the previous sections applies to teachers, for school is their workplace. The biblical models can be used as models for teaching. This next section is to help leaders think through the role the Bible can play in schools and the way in which our view of the Bible affects how it is used in the educational context. Christians work in schools in a number of capacities: schools workers, teachers, governors, volunteers. Some will be involved in classroom work and worship. Others will work at a level of policy, values and relationships. (Go to the following sites for resourcing governors and volunteers: www.stapleford-centre.co.uk, www.care.org.uk, www.natsoc.org.)

In some places the Bible will figure daily in schools: in other places it would be anathema for that to happen. Even in those places where the Bible is part of the curriculum, the experience of the Bible can vary greatly. For some pupils the experience of the Bible in school is creative, exciting and challenging; for others it is boring and manipulative, leaving them with the feeling that the adults use God or the Bible to prop up the school rules. How we use the Bible in schools is extremely important because for many people their only contact with the Bible may be in school and this could shape their attitude for life.

Reflection

Look at the cartoon below. How do you react to it? Did you ever experience anything like this as a child? What attitudes have your experiences of the Bible in the school left you with? How do you think they influenced your attitude to the Bible in later life? Think about a school you know. How do you think the children experience the Bible? How do you think the teachers experience the Bible? Record your thoughts in your reflective diary.

5. The difference between church and school

Worship in the school and church context are not the same, though superficial similarities can mask the differences. Both may have prayers and songs and use the Bible but in schools assent cannot be assumed and the authority of the Bible cannot be taken for granted. Biblical knowledge is likely to be low and pupils may come from all faiths and none. Reminding ourselves of the similarities and differences can help us use the Bible appropriately.

Activity 5 (I): Experiencing the Bible in different contexts

a. Think about your assumptions about the Bible and the way it is used in church. How would the change of context, from church to school, affect how you used the Bible? How would you adapt to the situation? Things to think about:

- ◆ the age of the children.
- ◆ their knowledge.
- ◆ their feelings about the Bible.
- ◆ the type of school (community, Church school).

b. People tend to concentrate on how they use the text rather than how pupils (and teachers) experience it. Look at the cartoon. What do you think the adult with the Bible is saying? Add a caption. Now add a thought bubble over the children's heads. What do you think they are thinking and feeling?

© Malcolm Laverty

Activity 5 (G)

Hold a caption competition, or pass the cartoon round and give the group paper speech and thought bubbles to fill in.

Feedback

a.

- ◆ I would still handle the Bible in a way that shows it is special to me. I would want to use one that looks attractive to children and suitable for the age group.
- ◆ Before using it with pupils I would try to look at the biblical material as if I had never heard it before and pick up any difficult ideas and language.
- ◆ I would be careful with the way I presented Bible stories prefacing them with sentences such as: 'Today we are having a story from the Bible that is important for Christians' so that the children and staff feel free to identify (or not) with what is being said rather than feeling that belief is being imposed on them.

b. My captions:

6. Approaches to using the Bible in school

Christian leaders are often are asked into schools to take part in RE lessons and there are many approaches available. Each uses the Bible in a different way. The three approaches sketched below are examples of those available, but they serve to show the way in which different views of the Bible result in different practice.

Activity 6 (I): Educational Pop Idol

As you read the case studies that follow, try to imagine the lessons described as entrants in a reality TV programme such as *Pop Idol*. Imagine the case study is a presentation of each approach that will be scored by judges. Score each out of ten for the following:

a. the basis on which stories are selected from the Bible (what is selected and why).
b. the way the Bible is presented and how engaging pupils would find it.
c. the pastoral possibilities in the way that the Bible is used.

Note: the same story has been used in each case so that you can see the impact of the different approaches.

Activity 6 (G)

As for the individual activity but spend some time discussing the approach first, then give people cards to fill in and hold up as score cards. They should justify their scoring.

Case study 1: A personal development approach

For some the Bible is a book that people can draw on to reach their full human potential. Approaches based on this view emphasise children's personal development and extending their emotional responses, rather than understanding religious concepts or increasing biblical knowledge. Material is selected from the Bible on the basis of the degree to which it addresses children's psychological needs.

At Lodge Road Infants School it is time for Religious Education. The teacher of the reception class (4–5 years) starts with some items in a bag that relate to the story, then she lights a story candle as a focus and tells the story of the Prodigal Son. She stops at intervals and blows the candle out, asks questions then relights the candle and continues. After the story is finished there is a discussion of repentance and forgiveness in which children explore their feelings about saying sorry. The children make sorry cards and there is time for the children to re-play the story using soft toys and to enact it taking different parts themselves. Dramatising the story encourages children to be drawn into it so that the story can address their concerns. Finally, they hear about Charlotte, a Christian child and what the story means to her.

This approach is exemplified in 'The Gift to the Child' (see the resources).

Case study 2: Concept and theme-based approaches

For some, the Bible is about the big ideas involved in our relationship with God; ideas such as sin, forgiveness and acceptance. Approaches based on this view emphasise understanding the basic themes and ideas (concepts) of the Bible and relating them to the pupils' lives rather than concentrating on passing on Bible knowledge or promoting personal development. For example, the concept of repentance might be demonstrated in a range of stories such as Zacchaeus and John the Baptist. Pupils would not need to know all the stories of repentance, just enough to understand the concept. This gives pupils a key to unlock other stories by themselves. Material from the Bible is selected on the basis that it helps to develop the pupils' understanding of the main theological themes of the Bible.

The students (ages 13–14) watched a video clip of a daughter returning home many years after she had run away. This was followed by a series of images of the Prodigal Son by artists from different times and cultures. As the images were shown, the teacher read the parable. The class then discussed key issues that the story raised: the Fatherhood of God, repentance and forgiveness. The class were given background information to help them understand the parable, then they imagined a modern prodigal son or daughter and were encouraged to think what they would feel like in that situation.

The class were able to choose from three activities:

a. creating a dance or a drama around the theme of leaving and returning and changing direction (repentance).

b. writing a poem or the lyrics to a song from the father's point of view exploring fatherhood.

c. creating a poster to capture the essence of forgiveness using text and images.

The session finished with some students presenting their work and one of the poems was read to the same images that were used at the beginning.

This approach is exemplified in 'Concept Cracking' and 'The Biblos Project' (see the resources).

Case study 3: Information-based approaches

For some the Bible is full of important information about God. Approaches based on this view of the Bible tend to stress learning biblical content, so material is selected from the Bible on the basis of what students need to know to have a good grasp of the Bible. This approach is reflected in syllabuses that systematically study the Old and New Testaments and Christianity as a phenomenon. This does not necessarily mean that concepts and personal development are ignored; it is a matter of emphasis.

For once the class of 12-year-olds were quiet as they created a storyboard of the parable of the Prodigal Son. The class liked this exercise and so did the teacher as it was easy to tell how much they had remembered. The class worked quickly as this left them time to do drama, which they really enjoyed. The drama involved groups composing their members into still scenes from the parable to create tableaux, and then photographing the tableaux with the digital camera. The pictures were put into the computer and a PowerPoint presentation was constructed with a commentary. At the end of the session, the teacher talked about the picture of God portrayed in the parable and asked the class to compare it with the way they imagined God. They were then tested on their knowledge of the story with a short quiz.

This approach is exemplified in the Request website www.request.org.uk

Feedback (extract)

I chose to score the developmental approach. I gave the developmental approach 8/10 for engagement and presentation, 9/10 for pastoral possibilities and 4/10 for selection, as the Bible is only seen as an instrument for pupils' development. I think this approach makes the text very real and relevant to children but if biblical material is only selected on this basis it could result in a very unrepresentative use of the text.

7. The Bible across the curriculum

The French language class worked in groups to create role plays using their new vocabulary. One half of the class used their vocabulary to demonstrate a shopping trip; the other half used the same words to welcome a stranger (in the biblical tradition of Deuteronomy 10:18–19). The latter role play was about a family from Rwanda who had arrived in the area as asylum seekers; the only way they could communicate was through French.

The Bible can impact on other areas of the curriculum – in this case study it is being used to change the emphasis in a modern languages session. The pupils are being encouraged to move from the language of tourism ('What can I get?') to the language of service ('How can I help?'). This is not about tagging a religious thought onto a basically secular subject. It's about creating stimulating activities that include a biblical perspective. For example, exploring number lines can stimulate discussions on infinity. Do numbers go on forever? For more information go to www.stapleford-centre.co.uk and search for the 'Charis Project'.

Activity 7 (I/G): The Bible shaping the curriculum

Choose three or more subjects from the curriculum and create questions that could open up discussion in which the Bible might play a part in some way. Look at the feedback for some examples.

Feedback

Here are my questions:

◆ *Maths*: What is the relationship between truth and statistics? (What does the Bible say about truth and honesty?)
◆ *Information Technology*: How do humans differ from computers? Can computers be good or evil? (What does the Bible say about the nature of people?)
◆ *Art*: Can you/should you represent God in art? (What does the Bible say about what God is like? Does the second commandment mean artists cannot represent God?)

Final Reflection

This unit has only been able to cover a small number of the issues raised when thinking about the use of the Bible in work and school contexts but you should now be able to go back to the key question and consider how you will answer it. Think about your overall response to the material in this unit and mark your response on the line. Are there other words that will encapsulate your response?

Excited————————————————————————————Nervous

Record your thoughts in your reflective diary.

Review

As a result of studying this unit you should now be able to:

◆ identify issues surrounding the use of the Bible in work and school contexts.
◆ explain how the Bible might shape aspects of the workplace.
◆ assess different approaches to using the Bible in schools.
◆ describe ways in which the Bible may contribute to the curriculum.

Resources

Cooling, T. (2003) *Rethinking: Try Something Different: Approaches to Teaching and Learning in RE.* The Stapleford Centre.

Cooling, T. and Cooling, M. (2004) *Rethinking: Concept Cracking: A Practical Way to Teach Big Ideas in RE.* Stapleford Centre.

Dadswell, C *et al.* (2003) *Making a Difference in your Community: Becoming a School Governor.* John Hunt Publishing.

Dadswell, C *et al.* (2002) *Becoming a Changeactivist School Governor.* CARE.

Farnell, A. *et al.* (2002) *Opening Windows: Spiritual Development in the Primary School.* The Stapleford Centre.

Greene, M. (1997) *Thank God It's Monday: Ministry in the Workplace* (second edition). Scripture Union.

Grimmit, M. *et al.* (1991) *The Gift to the Child: Religious Education in the Primary School.* Simon and Schuster.

Oliver, David. (2006) *Love Work Live Life.* Authentic.

Smith, D. I. and Shortt, J. (2002) *The Bible and the Task of Teaching.* The Stapleford Centre.

Smith, D. I. and Carvill, B. (2000) *The Gift of the Stranger: Faith, Hospitality and Foreign Language Learning.* Wm B. Eerdmans Publishing Co.

Volf, M. (2001) *Work in the Spirit Toward a Theology of Work.* Wipf and Stock Publishers.

www.encountersontheedge Select index and No 24 for information on workplace church

www.neafe.org. Select 'Saltley Trust' scroll down to 'Who am I and what am I doing?'

www.biblesociety.org.uk Search by 'Biblos' Project' for the books that resulted from this project. See also 'Transmission Spring 2006' on faith and work.

www.faithandtheworkplace.com

www.findarticles.com Search by 'The Bible and the workplace' using free articles

www.ekklesia.co.uk Search by 'schools'

www.rejesus.co.uk Explore the section called 'Sacred Space'. You may wish to evaluate this material

Unit 15

The Bible, the arts and pastoral practice

Key question
How might the arts enhance the use of the Bible in Christian ministry?

Preparation
This unit requires internet access, although books could be used instead, which might involve a trip to the library (page 145).

One group option includes bringing a book, poem, piece of music or image to share.

There is an option to watch a DVD.

1. Introduction

The research project revealed that some practitioners were integrating the use of the arts with their use of the Bible in Christian ministry. People were using film and painting, music and drama, poetry and writing. By far the most popular, however, was storytelling.

The arts have been used over the centuries to communicate the Bible and to make abstract ideas, such as faith, visible by clothing them in paint and story, movement and sound. For example, the medieval mystery plays communicated biblical stories and ideas by making them visible through drama. Churches make ideas visible in stone and glass. Music makes ideas audible in sound. Large parts of the Bible are also an artistic expression in their own right: poetry and song, drama and story. The arts do some of the work of interpreting the Bible (unit 5) by this re-clothing, providing, of course, that the art form is appropriate for the audience.

The arts have also a long history in pastoral work. By combining the Bible, the arts and the pastoral context, the creative possibilities multiply. The Beta course is a modern example of this (www.betacourse.org).

The arts can be used in a variety of church contexts and the particular context will govern the use; a film clip that would be inappropriate in a sermon could be appropriate in a housegroup. A poem that is right for a prayer group could be inappropriate for a basics group. The activities that follow do not stipulate the context as this can vary from church to church. In any context, understanding the biblical text is important. This can be done before it is expressed and interpreted artistically or the arts can be part of the process of understanding. For example, an artist's interpretation of a passage can make us look at a text again and aid our own understanding and interpretation.

In Christian ministry we deal with the big experiences of life that are sometimes beyond the ordinary use of words, and maybe beyond words altogether. Using the arts helps some people to express thoughts and feelings in these situations. For example, many people find that Barber's *Adagio for Strings* expresses grief in a way that words cannot. Having said this, how people react to the use of the arts in conjunction with the Bible varies; what moves one person leaves another untouched. This is not a reason for abandoning the arts; it is just a reminder that no approach is a panacea.

The arts can help us to reflect on life. When using the arts and the Bible to create an experience of the biblical text it is impossible to unpick such experiences and say how much is contributed by the Bible and how much by the arts. The arts and the text fuse to become a channel for the Spirit, as they do in the Psalms where poetry and text combine. Considering how the Bible, the arts and Christian ministry relate can open up creative ways of using the text.

Note: the word 'arts' is used to cover all major art forms not just 'art'. It is also applied to popular forms such as film, TV, computer design and photography.

Activity 1 (I): Making ideas and values visible

Think of one biblical idea: e.g. 'faith', 'peace', 'sacrifice' and search for an art form that would clothe that idea and make it communicable in a pastoral situation. For example, you could search the net for photographic images, or think of a film that captures that idea. You might want to use lyrics of a song, a piece of music or a book that you have read.

Useful websites

© Simon András

Visual images:
    www.istockphoto.com
    www.freeimages.co.uk
    www.allposters.co.uk
Music:
    www.essentialsofmusic.com
Films:
    see resources
Art:
    www.freeweb.hu/mkdsz1/simon.andras.galeria/indexa.html
    www.arttoheartweb.com www.hequiarts.com
    www.simongaleria./hu
see also resources section

Activity 1 (G)

As for the individual activity, but you may want to ask people to bring ideas and examples to share. This will involve doing some work before the group meets.

Feedback

I found this graphic that made me think about Jesus' sacrifice: 'The Chalice of Sacrifice' by Simon András (see above). The image of the crucifixion in the flower/chalice carries the ideas of both sacrifice and resurrection. The crucifixion in the black flower/cup made me think of the cup of suffering from the garden of Gethsemane and Christ's willing sacrifice. The upraised arms from the growing stalk and the white line around Jesus almost release him from the image of death and create a contrasting image of resurrection.

2. Helping people to engage

Carrie went to church but felt nothing; the words of the service simply went over her head, she had heard them many times before. In a time of quiet prayer the music group sang a scriptural song and a wave of emotion engulfed her as the music thawed her spirit. Words that had seemed pointless five minutes earlier suddenly felt as if they were spoken to her, and worship that she had been taking part in as a matter of form, suddenly became charged with meaning.

Think of a time you have sat through a church service feeling disengaged, where the words have meant little. Now think of a time when that changed and the service became meaningful. What caused the change? Have the arts ever played a role in bringing about that change for you? For some it happens when watching a drama or film, listening to or taking part in music or looking at images. Our over-familiarity with the text of the Bible, or just the numbness created by everyday life, can leave us disengaged. Sometimes it takes the arts to break through the numbness.

The arts also help us to engage with the text by approaching it from a fresh or indirect angle as in the case study that follows. Biblical stories can be read against the grain, from a minority perspective. For example, what would Hagar's perspective on Abraham and Sarah's story be? What would the brothers' perspective on Joseph's story have been? This technique is illustrated in the TV drama in the case study that follows, where the TV drama was based on the Good Samaritan, but focused on the passer-by. This technique can stimulate people to engage with the text, enabling them to see it afresh and feel its full impact.

The TV drama Passer-by *drew on the story of the Good Samaritan. It portrayed a nurse, known for his compassion, who failed to come to the aid of a woman who was being harassed on a train late at night. After the nurse left the train the woman was raped. He did not come forward as a witness as it meant admitting he had failed to help. The drama tracked his disintegration as a person who was unable to come to terms with what he had failed to do.*

Activity 2 (I): Seeing the story from a different perspective

Take a minor character or even create a character, and rethink a biblical story from their perspective. Make sure you stay with the meaning and main thrust of the text, but seen from another perspective. For example, what would the mother's reaction be in the story of the prodigal son?

Activity 2 (G)

As for the individual activity, but groups can do this as a drama. Some options:

◆ Hot-seating. This involves one person taking on the persona of a minor character and being questioned by the rest of the group. The person being 'hot-seated' must answer in role.

◆ A monologue from the minor/invented character's perspective.
◆ A line drama. The major characters stand in a line with a minor or invented character and they each wear labels saying who they are. Each comment, in turn, on the events and express their thoughts and feelings. They speak one after the other, speaking their lines expressively with gestures. See the feedback for an example.

Feedback

I tried to write a line drama for the prodigal son including the mother and found it surprisingly moving. Coming at the text from a different angle made me really look at the story again.

(extract)
PRODIGAL: I left them.
FATHER: I watched for him.
MOTHER: I grieved for them both.
PRODIGAL: I lived life to the full.
FATHER: I lived with fear for him.
MOTHER: I barely lived, my life went on hold.
PRODIGAL: I ate and drank to the full.
FATHER: Grief ate away at me.
MOTHER: I watched my other son eaten up with bitterness.

3. The use and misuse of the arts

History is littered with examples of the misuse of the arts, from Nazi sculptors and Communist posters to British imperial propaganda. Some advertisers have misused powerful images to sell their products. This has left some people wary of using the arts, not because they do not work, but because they work too well and there is a fear of manipulating others.

The arts communicate directly with our minds and emotions, rather than in ways that can be analysed and evaluated. They do this by using ways of knowing other than the logical/rational; instead they use symbol and metaphor, intuition and experience. This can be both an asset and a danger. C. S. Lewis referred to this ability of the arts as getting past the 'watchful dragons'. Another way of putting it would be getting under the radar of our conscious thoughts. Because the arts use ways of knowing that are felt and grasped rather than analysed, they can bypass our stereotypes and prejudices and help us to consider ideas we might otherwise dismiss. This facility also means that the arts can bypass the filters in our minds that alert us to ideas that are unhealthy or dangerous.

The arts do have to be handled carefully because they can move people, and we need to examine our motives for using them; is it to gain power and manipulate or is it for healing and wholeness? We also need to make sure that the emotions are not over-engaged for the intended purpose. Go to www.safeinchurch.co.uk for information on spiritual abuse.

Reflection

Have you ever experienced the arts being misused in a Christian context? Think about what made it misuse. Record your thoughts in your reflective diary.

4. 'Tell all the truth but tell it slant'

This quotation by the poet Emily Dickinson expresses the idea that the arts do not always tackle issues head on, they come at them 'slantwise'. The arts can be a more muted way of engaging an issue. For example, inviting someone to look at an image, film or poem that relates to the Bible and to their situation without directly addressing it may be more appropriate in some situations. The person can then take what they want from the experience. Some pastoral contexts can be highly charged and people can feel so tied up with their situation that it is difficult to gain any distance. Using the Bible directly in such a context may be inappropriate.

Activity 4 (I/G): The power of a painting

Read the biblical passages that follow and then look at the painting: 'Portrait of an old man and a young boy' by Domenico Ghirlandaio using one of the websites:

> www.barewall.com (search by 'old masters' then artist. This site has two posters, the original and one of the grandfather after plastic surgery!)
> www.abcgallery.com/G/ghirlandao/ghirlandaio.html
> www.sunsite.dk/ghirlandaio

Suggest ways in which this painting could be used 'slantwise' in a pastoral context. Select which texts that you might use with it. (You can use the ones on the list or suggest your own.)

Biblical passages:

> Isaiah 53
> Matthew 9:9–13
> Mark 1:40
> 1 Samuel 16:1–3

Some things to look for in the painting:

◆ body language and expression: what is being 'said'?
◆ dominant colour: what mood does it create?
◆ position: what is in the foreground, what is in the background? Why? What is in the centre?
◆ similarities and differences: compare and contrast the old man and the boy.

Feedback

I would use the painting on a quiet day. I would have different sessions that explored different aspects of the painting and text.

◆ For the first session I would look at modern images of male and female beauty. I would follow this by using both posters from the Barewall site and talk about the stress of physical perfection today (even the painting has had plastic surgery!). I would explore the idea of invisible ugliness and invisible beauty. I might use the story of *The Picture of Dorian Gray* as an illustration (www.awert.com/dorian2.html). I would bring out that God's love is not dependant on any sort of outward beauty, God looks inward (1 Samuel 16:1–3).
◆ For the second session I would look at Jesus' acceptance of sinners and the rejected people of society (Matthew 9:9–13, Mark 1:40). Many people would have rejected

the grandfather on the basis of his looks. God is not deterred by any inner ugliness.

◆ For the final session I would focus on Jesus as the suffering servant with no beauty (Isaiah 53).

5. A way of seeing

The arts, by creating worlds from sound, movement, image and words allow us to 'see'. We can look into these worlds and see people and situations from the outside while at the same time being drawn in. We might look at people in a novel or film and identify with them, deciding (often unconsciously) that we want to be like them or that we want to avoid their mistakes. The arts can help us do this with the Bible. For example, storytelling methods can make biblical narratives live and help us to identify with characters. Bible Society's video *Tales from the Madhouse* is a good example of this.

Some pastoral situations are the result of seeing the world in an unhelpful way. We might become aware that the problems presented are symptoms of a much deeper issue; for example, bitterness can be the result of expecting our experience of life to be perfect and seeing happiness as a right. In contrast the Bible sees this world as flawed, and not as God intended (Genesis 1–3). The arts can present a biblical way of seeing the world, revealing the beauty of creation, the depths of sin, the scope of redemption and the nature of love. Art that faces both the beauty and horror of this world does not seek to provide comfort alone; it also seeks to disrupt and challenge. An artist does not have to be a Christian to do this; films such as *The Shawshank Redemption* deal powerfully with suffering and redemption.

Reflection

Think of a time when you were challenged to see things differently, and more biblically, by the arts. It might have been a piece of music, or a painting, a photograph or a film. Record your thoughts in your reflective diary.

6. Focus and depth

Life is busy; many of us rush around and seldom stop to notice the world around us. Artists, photographers, musicians and poets can stop us in our tracks and make us notice. The poet might focus on one moment, one aspect of creation, one emotion. The artist or photographer might capture one glance, one flower, one interaction between two people. The musician might explore one feeling or event. Put such insights alongside the biblical text and the creative possibilities are endless. Such close-up attention allows us to see the depth of a relationship and the beauty of God's creation.

Activity 6 (I/G): Relating texts and the arts

Choose one or more of the following:

a. Read Matthew 6:24–34 and look at Georgia O'Keefe's flower paintings at www.georgiaokeefe.com . What do you notice that you do not normally see? Spend a few moments in prayer or reflection and record your thoughts.

b. Press the pause button when watching a film, focus on one glance or moment that you think communicates an important Christian (biblical) value and write a brief explanation.

c. Choose a Bible text and a piece of music that is appropriate as background for reading that text and explain your choice.

d. Look at the following extract from the poem *Remorse*, and put it alongside Luke 22:54–62 and write your response to the two texts.

Remorse by Emily Dickinson

Remorse is memory awake,
her parties all astir
a presence of departed acts
at window and at door.

Feedback

I chose Vaughan Williams' *Fantasia on a Theme by Thomas Tallis* as I thought it expressed the longing of Psalm 137.

7. A way to express ourselves

The arts facilitate us in expressing our thoughts and feelings concerning the Bible. For many, writing a poem, singing, designing a poster or a dance can be emotionally releasing expressions of our understanding of the Bible.

Activity 7 (I/G): Expression

Choose from the following:

a. A kenning is a device used in Norse and Anglo-Saxon forms of poetry. With kennings, things are often not named but their essential nature or role is expressed in short poetic phrases. For the Anglo Saxons the sea was 'the whale road', and the body was 'the bone-house'. Take a passage from the Gospels and create a kenning for Jesus based on that passage.

b. Take a biblical story and work through the following choices:

   ◆ choose a character from the story (e.g. Ruth).
   ◆ choose a time (e.g. 5pm).
   ◆ choose a place in the story appropriate to the character and time (e.g. a field).
   ◆ decide what the weather is like (e.g. very hot and dry).
   ◆ Choose a moment in the story (e.g. several months after she has promised to stay with Naomi).

c. Write in prose or poetry what you think the character in the story would have been thinking and feeling at that time and in those conditions.

d. Locate a song that expresses your understanding of a Bible passage. What is it about the song that captures the essence of the passage for you?

Feedback

I looked at the Resurrection stories and my kennings are: 'Tomb-cracker', 'Death defeater', 'Son riser'.

Final reflection

Return to the key question and answer it. Look back over this unit and identify two ways that you might now use the arts in your ministry. Identify one issue where you still feel unclear and would want to find out more. Record your thoughts in your reflective diary.

Review

As a result of studying this unit you should now be able to:

◆ articulate different ways in which the arts can encourage a creative use of the Bible in Christian ministry.
◆ discuss issues of the use and misuse of the arts.
◆ express key issues surrounding the use of the arts, the Bible and pastoral practice.

Resources

Ballard, P. and Holmes, S. R. (eds) (2005) *The Bible in Pastoral Practice*. Darton, Longman and Todd. Essays 17 and 18.

Brand, H. and Chaplin, A. (1999) *Art and Soul: Signposts for Christians in the Arts*. Solway.

Bond, F. (2001) *The Arts and Your Church: A Practical Guide*. Piquant.

Dury, J. (1999) *Painting the Word*. Yale University Press.

Ford, D. (ed.) (1997) *The Modern Theologians*. Blackwell Publishing Essays 34 (1) and 34 (2).

Harries, R. (1999) *Art and the Beauty of God: a Christian Understanding*. Mowbray.

Rookmaker, H. R. (1981) *The Creative Gift: The Arts and Christian Life*. Inter-Varsity Press.

Seerveld, C. (1988) *Rainbows for the Fallen world: Aesthetic Task and Artistic Life*. Stride.

Thistlethwaite, D. (1998) *The Art of God and the Religions of Art*. Solway.

www.damaris.org.uk films, books, music
www.reelissues.org.uk films
www.hollywoodjesus.com
www.rejesus.co.uk Select 'Expressions' for poetry and art
www.religion-online.org Select 'Culture'
www.moviesmatter.com
www.theoarts.org
www.st-andrews.ac.uk/institutes/itia/reading-lists/theoarts.html An extensive bibliography
www.christusrex.org
www.nationalgallery.org.uk

Section 4

The Next Step

Unit 16

Writing the next chapter: implementing your learning

We hope you have enjoyed analysing your ideas and assumptions about how the Bible could be used in pastoral practice as you have worked through this book. The book is designed to help you change how you think and act in relation to both the Bible and pastoral practice. So this final section is designed to help you to crystallise and summarise your learning, and to plan how you are going to put your hard work so far into practice. It will also help you to plan how you might go on to learn and develop more in the future. We have not provided many answers in this book, and we hope that you have enjoyed being 'co-author' by adding your own responses. The idea is that you continue to learn and reflect now that you have made a start here and carry on expressing your own understandings and commitments as you read further.

This final section is a time for looking back and reflecting on what you have learned. Think about the units you worked through and answer the questions that follow.

Reflection: Evaluating your learning

Spend a few moments thinking through the following areas and jotting down some notes:

◆ Look back at unit 3 (if you did this unit). Look at your definition of pastoral practice. Do you wish to change or modify your answer? Would you still define it in the same way?

Look through the notes you have made as you have worked through the book (you might find it useful to look at the index of activities on pages 157–9 to remind you of the overall shape and scope of the book and what you have done).

◆ What are the three main things you think you have learned about your use of the Bible and Christian ministry, and how will you gain from this?
◆ In what five main ways do you think your attitudes and thinking have changed?
◆ How does this thinking and attitudinal change affect your practice? Be specific about things you now do or might do differently, giving concrete examples if possible.
◆ Have you learned any new skills ? (Please remember that a book is not a good way of gaining practical skills, but you might have gained some anyway.)
◆ What do you think was your *biggest* gain from working through this book? Why?
◆ What was the *biggest* challenge you faced in working through it?
◆ What have you not learned or gained from it that you think you need to know or do? What might you do to remedy this by way of further work or study?
◆ Were there any ways in which the book disappointed you? Be specific.

One way of further concretising and crystallising your learning is to ask you now to identify for yourself principles of good and poor practice in using the Bible in pastoral practice. (You may wish to refer back to your thoughts on good practice if you did unit 1.)

Activity: Good and bad practice in using the Bible in ministry

Imagine you are mentoring someone just starting in Christian ministry. How would you define good practice concerning the use of the Bible? Create your own code of good practice. It might help you to sharpen this if you express it in two lists of do's and don'ts.

Another way of ensuring that you translate ideas and concepts into action and further learning is to invite you to create your own action plan for the immediate future.

Using the Bible in Ministry: Personal Action Plan

Knowledge and skills need using, enhancing, updating and disseminating. Once we have learned something, we need to think about what we will do with it. One way of ensuring this is to create an action plan; this involves setting short, medium and long-term goals.

Short-term goals

Think of something you could do to enhance, use or disseminate the knowledge and skills you have gained within the next six weeks, something that is realistic and achievable in the time. Put up a post-it note where you will see it and make a note in your diary. At the end of the six weeks, check that you have achieved your goal. You can set other short term goals if you wish.

Medium-term goals

Think of something that is more difficult to achieve in terms of use, enhancement or dissemination that will take around six months. Again, choose something appropriate for the time scale and the commitments you have. Put up a post-it note where you will see it and make a note in your diary. At the end of six months revisit your goal to see if you have achieved it.

Long-term goals

A long-term goal could take one or two years. Some are even longer, but it is easier to keep track of goals that do not disappear into the distant future, so stick with one or two years. Think what you want to do long-term with the results of reading this book. What long-term changes to you want to make? Set realistic goals and devise a regular reminder so that you stay on track. This could be done as a chart.